Electric Pressure Cooker Recipes

Over 100 Delicious Quick And Easy Recipes For Fast Meals

RONNIE ISRAEL

ISBN-13:978-1511726993

ISBN-10:1511726997

DEDICATION

To all those who love to cook.

TABLE OF CONTENTS

INTRODUCTION

To a lot of people, cooking is a tedious and time consuming activity, especially if the desired result is a really good meal. They cannot spare the time required for the preparations. The good news is that pressure cookers help to prepare wonderfully delicious foods in ways that save time and effort. They make use of high pressures and high temperatures to expedite the cooking activity and at the same time, retaining the nutritious content of the foods.

With pressure cooker, you may only need to spend 30 minutes or less in cooking but going the traditional way may take hours. Pressure cookers are just right for those occasions when you have to do other chores around the house or away from it. The stovetop isn't always practical even for those who are skilled at multitasking. At these times, an electric pressure cooker is the more practical solution.

While pressure cookers aren't new phenomenon, today's pressure cookers are much safer and easier to use. They also last longer, are extremely versatile and designed to save energy. You can use electric pressure cookers to sauté, steam, braise, fry or just to warm your food.

In fact, almost anything can be cooked in your electric pressure cooker, which is why I have put together over 100 delicious recipes that you can try your hands on. If you love food and flavors, you do not need to spend hours cooking them.

So add more culinary joy to your life by trying the recipes in this book. With easy, quick- to prepare recipes consisting of chicken, pork, beef, soups, stews, desserts and lots more, you will definitely enjoy cooking with your electric pressure cookers.

Pressure Cooker Pork Recipes

Pork Loin Dinner

With this dish, you can cook everything up in one pot. Serve this delicious dinner with a tossed salad and warm buttered dinner rolls.

Servings: 4

<u>Ingredients</u>

1 pound pork loin, boneless

4 small Yukon Gold or red potatoes, scrubbed, cut into quarters

1 small onion, peeled & diced

1 tablespoon vegetable oil

½ cup apple juice or white wine

1 cup chicken broth

1 large turnip, peeled & diced

1 rutabaga, peeled & diced

½ teaspoon mild curry powder

1 stalk celery, finely diced

¼ teaspoon dried thyme

4 carrots, peeled and diced

½ cup sliced leeks, white part only

2 teaspoons dried parsley

3 tablespoons fresh lemon juice

2 tart green or Granny Smith apples, peeled, cored& diced

Salt and freshly ground black pepper, to taste

Fresh parsley or thyme sprigs, optional

Preparation

1. Add oil to pressure cooker. Bring to temperature over medium heat. Next, add the onion; sauté 3 minutes. Add the pork and season lightly with salt and pepper. Stir-fry pork for 5 minutes.

2. Add the apple juice or wine, broth, turnip and rutabaga. Add the potatoes to the pot along with the celery, carrots, curry powder, leeks, parsley, lemon juice and thyme.

3. Secure lid and bring to high pressure; maintaining this pressure for 15 minutes. Turn heat off and allow the pressure to drop of its own accord.

4. Remove the lid carefully and add the diced apples. Bring to a simmer over medium heat; lower heat and simmer covered for 5 minutes. Serve in large bowls, garnished with thyme or fresh parsley.

Roast Pork With Sweet Potatoes & Cinnamon Cranberries
Serve this dish with steamed vegetables, a tossed salad and dinner rolls.

Servings: 6

Ingredients

3 large sweet potatoes, peeled & quartered

1 3-pound pork butt roast

¼ cup orange marmalade

1 16-ounce can sweetened whole cranberries

1 medium onion, peeled& diced

½ cup orange juice

1/8 teaspoon ground cloves

¼ teaspoon ground cinnamon

1 tablespoon cornstarch, optional

2 tablespoons cold water, optional

Salt freshly ground pepper, to taste

Preparation

1. In the pressure cooker, place the pork, fat side down and add salt and pepper to taste. Mix together the cranberries, marmalade, onion, cinnamon, cloves and orange juice in a large measuring cup and pour over the pork roast.

2. Arrange the quartered sweet potatoes around the meat. Close lid securely and bring to low pressure for 45 minutes. Remove from heat and let pressure release.

3. Remove meat and sweet potatoes to a platter. Cover and keep warm. Skim off fat from the pan juices.

4. Return the pressure cooker to medium heat. Add cornstarch and water together. Whisk into the liquid in the pressure cooker. Next, simmer and stir for 2 minutes.

Pork/Beans Delight

Servings: 6

Ingredients

2½ pounds pork shoulder, cut into 1½ inch pieces

2 cups dried white beans

1 15-ounce can diced tomatoes

2 teaspoons paprika

¼ teaspoon ground black pepper

1 teaspoon garlic powder

½ teaspoon onion powder

¼ teaspoon dried oregano

1/8 teaspoon cayenne

¼ teaspoon dried thyme

½ cup packed light brown sugar

1 large yellow onion, peeled &diced

1½ tablespoons vegetable oil

6 cups chicken broth or water

½ pound salt pork or bacon, cut into pieces

4 cloves garlic, peeled and minced

2 teaspoons chili powder

1 bay leaf

¼ teaspoon salt

¼ teaspoon dried thyme

2 tablespoons whole grain or Creole mustard

Preparation

1. Add the garlic powder, paprika, onion powder, pepper, cayenne, thyme and oregano to a plastic bag and shake to mix. Add the pieces of pork and shake the bag to season the meat well.

2. Add the vegetable oil to the pressure cooker, bring to temperature over medium-high heat and add the pork, stir-frying for about 2 minutes on each side or until it just starts to brown. Transfer meat to a plate and then set aside.

3. Add the onions to the pressure cooker; lower heat to medium and sauté until tender. Add the water or broth.

4. Remove any impurities or stones from the beans; stir them into the liquid in the cooker, while scraping up browned bits off the pot bottom. (Browned bits on the pan bottom may burn during the pressure process and impart an unpleasant burnt flavor to the resulting dish.)

5. Close lid on the pressure cooker. Bring to high pressure for 15 minutes. Turn burner off; leave pressure cooker in place until it goes back to normal pressure. Remove the lid once the pressure is released so excess steam can escape.

6. (If the meat or beans aren't tender enough, cover and simmer again for 15 minutes more or lock the lid, return to high pressure, and cook at high pressure for 3 more minutes).

7. Add the tomatoes, garlic, salt pork, mustard, thyme, light brown sugar, chili powder, bay leaf, reserved pork and salt to the cooker; stir. Lock the lid; bring pressure cooker to high pressure for 15 minutes.

6. Take it out from heat and set aside for 10 minutes. Quick-release any left-over pressure and remove the lid. If needed, add salt and pepper. Remove and throw out the bay leaf.

Raisin Sauced Ham

Serve with a salad, sweet potatoes, a steamed vegetable and dinner rolls.

Servings: 8

Ingredients

1 4-pound ham (ready-to-eat)

1 large sweet onion, peeled & sliced

¼ teaspoon ground ginger

1/8 teaspoon ground cloves

¼ cup maple syrup

1 14-ounce can pineapple chunks

½ teaspoon ground cinnamon

½ cup raisins

2 tablespoons brown sugar

1 tablespoon balsamic vinegar

½ cup apple butter

Preparation

1. Add the sliced onions and ham to the pressure cooker. Combine the cinnamon, ginger, cloves, brown sugar, raisins and pineapple juice and pour over the ham.

2. Cover lid securely. Bring to low pressure for 20 minutes. Remove from heat and let the pressure release naturally.

3. Transfer the ham to a serving plate and keep warm. Skim and remove fat from the pan juices. Put the pan in the pressure cooker over medium heat; simmer to lessen the pan juices to about 1 cup.

4. Stir in the maple syrup, pineapple chunks, vinegar and apple butter. Taste for seasoning and adjust accordingly. (If you want a sweeter sauce, add more maple syrup; if you need to cut the sweetness, add more vinegar)

5. Pour over ham slices.

BBQ Western Ribs

For a delicious, casual meal, add potato chips and coleslaw.

Servings: 4

Ingredients

1 3-inch cinnamon stick

3 pounds pork Western ribs

1 cup barbeque sauce

6 whole cloves

½ cup apple jelly

½ cup water

1 large sweet onion, peeled & diced

Preparation

1. Add the cinnamon stick, barbeque sauce, cloves, water, onion and jelly to the pressure cooker and stir.

2. Add the ribs, spooning some sauce over them. Secure lid into place, bring to low pressure and maintain pressure for 55 minutes. Take away from heat and let the pressure release naturally.

3. Remove the bones and meat; cover and keep warm. Skim fat from sauce. Remove cloves and cinnamon stick and return the pressure cooker to medium-high temperature.

4. Cook uncovered until the sauce is lessened and coats the back of a spoon.

5. (To stretch this recipe to 8 servings, serve barbeque pork sandwiches rather than 4 servings of pork).

German Pork Chops & Sauerkraut

Servings: 4

Ingredients

1 1-pound bag baby carrots

1 stalk celery, finely chopped

1 large onion, peeled & sliced

1 12-ounce can beer

4 slices bacon, cut into small pieces

1 clove garlic, peeled & minced

4 1-inch-thick bone-in pork loin chops

4 medium red potatoes, peeled & quartered

1 1-pound bag sauerkraut, rinsed & drained

2 teaspoons Bavarian seasoning

Salt & freshly ground pepper, to taste

Preparation

1. Add the stalk, carrot, onion, garlic, bacon, pork loin chops, sauerkraut, potatoes, beer, Bavarian seasoning, salt and pepper to the pressure cooker. Lock lid and bring to high pressure for 9 minutes.

2. Remove from heat and let the pressure release on its own. If necessary, add more seasoning. Serve hot.

Flavorful Pork Roast
Servings: 8 to 10

Ingredients

1 tbsp vegetable oil

1 3-pound boneless pork loin

5 cloves minced garlic

1 cup white wine or water

1 tbsp lemon juice

1 tbsp chopped fresh rosemary

1 tsp grated lemon zest

1/2 tsp dried thyme leaves

1 tbsp olive oil

1/2 cup water

1/2 tsp salt

1/4 tsp pepper

<u>Preparation</u>

1. Pour vegetable oil into the pressure cooker. Set it to Brown and let the oil heat.

2. Now add pork roast and brown the meat on all sides evenly.

3. Meanwhile, place rosemary, garlic, thyme, lemon zest, salt, pepper, olive oil and lemon juice in a small bowl, mixing well.

4. Remove the browned pork roast from the cooker and set aside. Place the meat rack in the cooker and water and wine.

5. Place the browned pork roast on meat rack. With a pastry brush, brush sides and top of roast with the rosemary mixture.

6. Cover and let it cook at High Pressure for 60 minutes.

7. Release pressure quickly.

Balsamic Pork Chops& Figs

Serve with a tossed salad, baked potatoes, steamed vegetable and topwith toasted walnuts and diced apples.

Servings: 4

<u>Ingredients</u>

½ cup chicken broth

10 ounces dried figs

4 1-inch-thick bone-in pork loin chops

2 teaspoons ghee or butter

2 medium sweet onions, peeled & sliced

2 teaspoons extra virgin olive oil

4 cloves garlic, peeled & minced

3 tablespoons balsamic vinegar

½ teaspoon dried thyme

2 tablespoons dry white wine

Salt & freshly ground black pepper, to taste

<u>Preparation</u>

1. Season the pork chops lightly on both sides by sprinkling with salt & pepper. Add the oil and ghee or butter to the pressure cooker and bring over medium-high heat.

2. Add 2 pork chops; brown on each side for 3 minutes. Transfer chops to a platter and repeat with the remaining 2 chops. Transfer those chops to the platter.

3. Add the onions; sautéing for 4 minutes then stir in the garlic and sautéing for 30 seconds. Stir in the balsamic vinegar and thyme. Cook uncovered until vinegar is lessened by half.

4. Stir in the broth and wine. Add the pork chops, spoon some onions over the chops and place the figs on top. Secure lid and bring to high pressure for 9 minutes. Remove from heat and quickly release the pressure. Serve immediately.

<u>Make a Syrupy Sauce</u>

1. Using a slotted spoon, transfer the onions, pork chops, and figs to a serving plate; cover and keep warm. Bring back the pressure cooker to medium-high heat.

2. Simmer, uncovered until the pan juices are lessened and coat the back of a spoon.

3. Next, pour over the figs, onions and pork chops on the serving platter.

Almost Sweet Pork
Serve over Chinese noodles or cooked. Place soy sauce and toasted sesame oil at the table.

Servings: 8

Ingredients

1 tablespoon all-purpose flour

2 pounds pork shoulder, cut into bite-size pieces

1 14-ounce can pineapple chunks

2 tablespoons peanut or sesame oil

1/8 teaspoon mustard powder

1 tablespoon light brown sugar

½ teaspoon ground ginger

1 tablespoon low-sodium soy sauce

2 tablespoons apple cider vinegar

1 large red bell pepper, seeded & sliced

4 medium carrots, peeled & sliced

½ pound fresh sugar snap peas

2 cloves garlic, peeled & thinly sliced

2 cups fresh broccoli florets, cut into bite-size pieces

2 large sweet onions, peeled & diced

14

2 tablespoons cornstarch

1 cup bean sprouts

2 tablespoons cold water

<u>Preparation</u>

1. Add the pork pieces to a zip-closure bag and add the flour; seal and shake to coat the pork.

2. In the pressure cooker, bring the oil to temperature over medium-high heat. Fry the pork for 3 minutes. Add the pineapple juice (reserve the pineapple chunks); mix well, scraping up any bits stuck to the pan bottom.

3. Add the mustard powder, sugar, vinegar, ginger, carrots, Liquid Aminos or soy sauce, sugar snap peas and red bell pepper.

4. Add the broccoli florets to the pressure cooker. Add ¾ onion and garlic. Close lid and bring to low pressure for 12 minutes. Release pressure quickly.

5. With a slotted spoon, transfer all the solids in pressure cooker to a serving platter; keep warm.

6. To make the glaze, combine the cornstarch and water in a small bowl. Add some of the pan juices and stir. Set pressure cooker to medium heat, bring to a boil and then stir in the cornstarch mixture.

7. Lower the heat until the mixture thickens and the raw cornstarch taste is cooked. Add the bean sprouts, onion and reserved pineapple chunks and stir. Pour over the vegetables and cooked pork in the serving platter; stir to mix.

Pork Chops In Marsala

Servings: 4

Ingredients

2 tbsp all-purpose flour

1/4 cup Italian seasoned bread crumbs

6 tbsp grated Parmesan cheese, divided

4 boneless pork chops, about 3/4 to 1-inch thick

1 package (8-ounces) sliced mushrooms

3/4 cup Marsala wine

1 tbsp vegetable oil

2 cloves garlic, minced

2 tbsp butter or margarine

1/2 teaspoon salt

1/2 teaspoon pepper

Preparation

1. Combine 1/4 cup Parmesan cheese, flour, bread crumbs, salt and pepper in a bowl.

2. Coat each pork chop liberally with bread crumb mixture and set aside.

3. Pour vegetable oil into the pressure cooker. Set it to Brown and let the oil heat.

4. Add garlic and sauté for 2 minutes. Add the pork chops and brown the meat evenly on both sides. Transfer chops to platter and set aside.

5. Add the butter to pressure cooker and melt. Sauté mushrooms for 3- 5 minutes. Add the Marsala wine to mushrooms, stirring well.

6. Place the pork chops on top of the mushrooms. Cover and cook for 8 minutes at High Pressure. Quickly release pressure.

7. Transfer pork chops to serving plate.

8. If you want your Marsala sauce to be thicker, cook the mushroom sauce, uncovered, at Brown, until it is thicker. Serve sauce over pork chops and sprinkle the remaining 2 tablespoons Parmesan cheese.

Sausages With Green Peppers & Sautéed Onions
Serve this recipe in steamed or toasted sandwich rolls.

Servings: 8

<u>Ingredients</u>

8 Italian sausages, 8 bratwurst or16 breakfast sausage links

½ cup chicken broth

1 large green bell pepper, seeded & sliced

1 large orange bell pepper, seeded & sliced

1 large red bell pepper, seeded& sliced

2 large sweet onions, peeled & sliced

1 large yellow bell pepper, seeded & sliced

2 cloves garlic, peeled & minced

1 tablespoon olive oil

<u>Preparation</u>

1. Brown sausages in pressure cooker over medium-high heat. Drain fat and discard. Add the olive oil and bring to temperature.

2. Next, add the peppers and sauté for 3 minutes. Add the onion slices and sauté until the onions are transparent. Add the garlic; sautéing again for 30 seconds.

3. Bring the sausages back to the pressure cooker; push them down into the onions and peppers. Pour in the broth. Close lid and bring to high pressure for 4 minutes. Quickly release the pressure.

Fruit Sauced Pork Steak

Serve over mashed potatoes and some steam-in-the-bag green beans.

Servings: 6

Ingredients

8 pitted prunes

4 8-ounce pork steaks, trimmed of fat

2 small Granny Smith apples, peeled, cored& sliced

½ cup heavy cream

½ cup dry white wine or apple juice

1 tablespoon red currant jelly

1 tablespoon butter, optional

Salt and freshly ground pepper, to taste

Preparation

1. Add the pork steaks, prunes, apple slices, cream and apple juice or wine to the pressure cooker.

18

2. Add salt and pepper to taste. Secure lid and bring to high pressure for 9 minutes. Quickly release the pressure. Transfer meat and fruit to a platter.

3. Do not remove the pressure cooker from the heat but simmer uncovered for 10 minutes.

4. Once mixture reduces by half and thickens, whisk in the red currant jelly. Add more salt and pepper if necessary. If you prefer a richer, glossier sauce, whisk in the butter 1 teaspoon at a time.

Pressure Cooker Beef & Meat Recipes

Fav Corned Beef & Cabbage

Servings: 4- 6

<u>Ingredients</u>

2 large red potatoes, cut into 2-inch chunks

1 medium head cabbage, cut into 8 wedges

1 medium onion, cut into 2-inch pieces

1 can (14-1/2 ounces) chicken broth

1 corned beef brisket & spice packet (2 pounds)

4 large carrots, cut into 2-inch chunks

4 cups water

<u>Preparation</u>

1. Add water and the corned beef seasoning packet together in a pressure cooker; add beef. Cover securely. Set to high pressure and cook for 45 minutes.

2. Meanwhile, combine the potatoes, cabbage and broth in a large saucepan and bring to a boil. Lower heat; cover and simmer for up to 10 minutes. Add onion and carrots. Cover and simmer for 20-25 minutes more or until the vegetables are tender; drain.

3. Release pressure. Move beef to a serving dish. Discard the cooking liquid. Serve beef with potatoes, cabbage, onion and carrot.

North African Lamb Tajine

Servings: 4-6

Ingredients

2.5 -3 lbs lamb shoulder, cut into pieces

1 teaspoon cinnamon powder

1 teaspoon ginger powder

1 teaspoon turmeric powder

1 teaspoon cumin powder

2 garlic cloves, crushed

2 onions, roughly sliced

10 oz or 300g prunes, soaked or a mixture of dry raisins and apricots

3.5 oz (100g) Almonds, shelled, peeled & toasted

1 bay leaf

1 cinnamon stick

1 cup vegetable stock

3 tablespoon honey

Salt & pepper to taste

Olive oil

Sesame seeds

Preparation

1. Combine the ground cinnamon, ginger, garlic, turmeric with 2 spoons of olive oil to form a paste. Cover meat with this paste and then set aside. In a

bowl, place the dried prunes and pour boiling water over them, cover and set aside.

2. Pre-heat the cooker, add onions and 2 swirls of olive oil and cook 3 minutes until softened. Pour the onions out and set aside.

3. Next, add the meat and for about 10 minutes brown, on all sides. Deglaze the pressure cooker with the vegetable stock (scrape the bottom thoroughly and incorporate any brown bits into the sauce). Now, add the bay leaf, onions and cinnamon stick.

4. Secure lid. Cook for 35 minutes and then add the honey, the rinsed and drained prunes. Sauté and simmer for 5 minutes. Discard the cinnamon stick and bay leaf.

5. Sprinkle with sesame seeds and toasted almonds and serve.

Beef Shank With Kikkoman Light Soy Sauce

Servings: 6

<u>Ingredients</u>

1000 g Beef shank

Marinate ingredients:

3 tbsp Kikkoman light soy sauce

2 tsp pepper cones

1 tsp salt

1 tsp sugar

Sauce ingredients:

2 tsp sugar

2 tsp salt

1/2 cup Kikkoman light soy sauce

3 clovers

3 tbsp dark soy sauce

2 anises

1.5 tsp cumin

1 tbsp Jasmine green tea

2 bay leaves

2 tsp sesame oil

2 chopped green onion

5g fresh ginger shredded

5 cups water

Preparation

1. Put the beef shank, light soy sauce, pepper cones, salt and sugar (the marinate ingredients) in a Zip-Lock bag, seal, shake thoroughly and refrigerate for1 day.

2. Rinse pepper cones. Place beef shank with all ingredients in the pressure cooker. Close the lid and set to 35 minutes of cooking time.

3. Wait another 10 minutes, re-lease the pressure slowly and open the lid. Remove the cooked beef shank and place on a bowl. Chill for 4 hours, slice and serve.

Savory Enchiladas

To make this recipe a one-dish meal, serve it over shredded lettuce and top it with chopped green onion, sour cream and some guacamole.

Servings: 8

<u>Ingredients</u>

1 large onion, peeled & diced

2 cups refried beans

2 pounds lean ground beef

1 12-ounce jar mild enchilada sauce

1 4½-ounce can chopped chilies

1 10½-ounce can golden mushroom soup

1 10½ ounce can cream of mushroom soup

1 10½-ounce can Cheddar cheese soup

1 10½-ounce can cream of celery soup

Plain corn tortilla chips, to taste

<u>Preparation</u>

1. Add the diced onion and ground beef to the pressure cooker. Set to high pressure and maintain for 5 minutes.

2. Quickly release the pressure and remove lid. Take out and discard any fat. Add the ground beef to the onions, stirring and breaking the beef apart.

3. Stir in enchilada sauce, chilies and refried beans soups. Secure lid into place. Bring to low pressure for 5 minutes.

4. If serving immediately, quick release the pressure. If not, remove from the heat and let the pressure release on its own.

5. Stir 8 ounces tortilla chips or more into the mixture in the pressure cooker. Cover, stir for 15 minutes over medium-low heat or until the tortilla chips softens.

Kielbasa, Kraut & Cabbage
Servings: 4

Ingredients

1 pound smoked, well cooked sausage or Kielbasa, cut into 2-inch pieces

1 can (16 ounces) sauerkraut, drained

1 bacon, sliced, cut into 1/2-inch pieces

3 cups shredded green cabbage

1 onion, chopped

1 tablespoon brown sugar

1/4 teaspoon celery seed

1 cup water

1 teaspoon salt

1/4 teaspoon pepper

Preparation

1. Place the bacon in the pressure cooker and set to Brown, sautéing bacon for 3 minutes.

2. Add onion and sauté for 3 to 4 minutes more or until bacon is just crisp and the onion is tender.

3. Add remaining ingredients and stir. Cover and cook for 5 minutes at High Pressure. Release pressure quickly.

Granny Pot Roast

Servings: 8

<u>Ingredients</u>

1 3-pound boneless chuck roast

2 stalks celery, diced

1 1-pound bag of baby carrots

1 large yellow onion, peeled & sliced

1 green bell pepper, seeded &diced

1 envelope onion soup mix

1 cup tomato juice

½ teaspoon black pepper

2 cloves garlic, peeled & minced

1 tablespoon steak sauce

1 tablespoon Worcestershire sauce

1 cup water

<u>Preparation</u>

1. Cut the roast into serving-sized portions. Add the celery, green bell pepper, onion and carrots, to the pressure cooker.

2. Place the roast pieces on the vegetables and sprinkle with black pepper and soup mix.

3. Add the garlic, steak, Worcestershire sauce, tomato juice and water to a bowl; mix thoroughly and then pour into the pressure cooker.

4. Close lid and bring to low pressure for 45 minutes. Remove from heat and let the pressure release naturally.

5. (This meal can be turned into 2 meals for 4 people the next day by making roast beef sandwiches. Refrigerating the leftovers in the pan juices will make the meat moist and tender).

Braised Barbecued Ribs In Beer
Servings: 2-4

Ingredients

2-1/2 pounds country-style pork ribs

2 cloves garlic, minced

1 onion, sliced

1 cup beer

1/4 cup Dijon mustard

1-1/2 cups barbecue sauce

1 bay leaf

1 teaspoon salt

1/2 teaspoon pepper

1 whole clove

1/4 cup brown sugar

Preparation

1. Place the ribs in the pressure cooker. Add garlic, onion, beer and seasonings. Cover and cook 30 minutes at High Pressure. Gradually release pressure.

2. Scoop out all but leave about 1/2 cup of beer and drippings. Take away and discard clove and bay leaf.

3. Combine sugar, mustard and barbecue sauce and pour over ribs. Cover and cook 10 minutes at High Pressure 10 minutes. Gradually release pressure.

Mixy Meatballs

Servings: 4

Ingredients

2/3 cup Rice, uncooked

1 1/2 lbs. Hamburger

2 tsp. Minced Onion, dry

1 tsp. Salt

1/2 tsp. Pepper

1 Can Tomato Soup

1/2 Cup Water

Preparation

1. Combine the hamburger, onion, rice, salt and pepper & form into small balls.

2. Next mix the soup and water and heat mixture in the Pressure Cooker. Drop the formed meat balls into hot soup mixture.

3. Close firmly with pressure regulator on top. Cook at high pressure for 10 minutes. Let pressure drop naturally.

Rich Barbecued Beef

Serve beef barbeque over cooked pasta. Top with grated Cheddar cheese and diced green or sweet onion.

Servings: 8

Ingredients

1 3-pound beef English roast

1 tablespoon red wine vinegar

½ cup red wine

2 teaspoons Worcestershire sauce

½ cup ketchup

2 teaspoons mustard powder

1 teaspoon dried minced garlic

2 tablespoons dried minced onion

1 teaspoon cracked black pepper

Pinch dried crushed pepper flakes

1 teaspoon chili powder

1 tablespoon brown sugar

½ teaspoon ground cinnamon

¼ teaspoon ground ginger

¼ teaspoon ground cloves

Pinch ground allspice

1 cup water

Preparation

1. Cut the roast into two and stack in the pressure cooker. Combine the rest of the ingredients and then pour mixture over the beef.

2. Close cover securely, bringing to low pressure 55 minutes. Take out from the heat and allow pressure to drop on its own.

3. Remove beef from cooker with a slotted spoon; pull beef apart, discard any gristle or fat. Taste the sauce and meat and if necessary, adjust seasonings.

4. Return pressure cooker to heat to thicken the sauce. Skim fat off the surface of the sauce. Simmer uncovered. Stir so the sauce doesn't burn.

Shredded Beef &Burrito Filling

For more heat, use jalapeño, panilla, poblano or Anaheim peppers instead of the green pepper and use hot enchilada sauce as well.

Servings: 6

Ingredients

1 large green bell pepper, seeded &diced

1 large sweet onion, peeled & diced

1 10-ounce can enchilada sauce

30

1 3-pound English roast or beef brisket

¼ cup water

Preparation

1. Add the enchilada sauce, onion and green pepper to the pressure cooker. Add the water. Trim any fat from the roast and discard.

2. Place the roast in the pressure cooker. Lock the lid and set to low pressure; maintaining this pressure for 50 minutes. Take out from heat and let the pressure release on its own.

2. Transfer the meat to a cutting board and then shred it. Put the shredded beef back into the sauce in the pressure cooker. Return pan to medium heat; simmer uncovered for 3-4 minutes to bring the meat back up to pressure and thicken the sauce.

3 Peppered Round Steak
Ingredients

1-1/2 pounds beef round steak, boneless, cut 1/2-inch thick

1 small red pepper, cut into strips

1 can (14.5 ounces) diced tomatoes

1 jalapeno pepper, seeded and minced

2 tablespoons vegetable oil, divided

1/2 cup salsa

1 teaspoon paprika

1 medium onion, sliced

1 small green pepper, cut into strips

31

1 teaspoon seasoned salt

1 tablespoon Worcestershire sauce

1/4 cup water

Preparation

1. Cut the steak into 4 to 6 serving pieces and then sprinkle with paprika and salt.

2. Pour 1 tablespoon of oil into the pressure cooker. Set it to Brown and let the oil heat. Add steak, in small quantities and brown meat on both sides evenly. Set aside browned beef.

3. Pour the rest of the oil into the pressure cooker and leave to heat. Add onions and sauté, stirring for 3 minutes.

4. Place half of the meat over the onions. Spoon about half of the tomatoes over steak and then top it with the remaining steak, tomatoes, peppers and salsa.

5. Blend the Worcestershire sauce into water, pour over meat and cover, cooking at high for 15 minutes. Gradually release pressure.

Southern- Style Beef Roll-Ups
Servings: 6

Ingredients

1-1/2 pounds beef round steak, boneless, cut into 1/2 x 2-inch slices

1 can (15 ounces) black beans, rinsed & drained

1 teaspoon vegetable oil

1 small green pepper, thinly sliced

1 onion, thinly sliced

1 small red pepper, thinly sliced

1 teaspoon cumin

2 teaspoons chili powder

6 (8-inch) flour tortillas, warmed

1 can (14-1/2 ounces) stewed tomatoes, Mexican flavored

Toppings: chopped green onion, sour cream, chopped tomatoes, shredded Cheddar cheese

Preparation

1. Pour vegetable oil into the pressure cooker. Set it to Brown and let oil heat. Add the beef and brown for 3 to 5 minutes.

2. Add peppers and onion and sauté for 3 minutes. Add cumin, chili powder, black beans and stewed tomatoes.

3. Cover and cook15 minutes on High Pressure. Gradually release pressure.

4. Remove beef mixture using a slotted spoon and place in tortillas. Now garnish with toppings.

Braised Meat Meal

To get thick gravy, thicken the pan juices with a cornstarch or roux.

Servings: 6

Ingredients

6 medium white potatoes, scrubbed

2½ pounds of beef round steak, 1-inch thick

1 cup tomato juice

6 large carrots, peeled

1 tablespoon vegetable oil

1 medium yellow onion, peeled and diced

2 stalks celery, diced

1 cup beef broth or water

1 large green pepper, seeded and diced

Salt and freshly ground pepper, to taste

4 teaspoons butter, optional

Preparation

1. Cut steak into 6 pieces. Add the oil and then bring it to temperature over medium heat. Season the meat with salt and pepper on both sides.

2. Now add 3 pieces of the seasoned meat and fry on each side for 3 minutes to brown them. Transfer to a platter and do the same with the remaining 3 pieces of meat.

3. Leave the last browned meat pieces in the cooker; add the green pepper, celery and onion on top of them.

4. Place the other 3 pieces of meat and pour the water or broth and tomato juice over them. Place the potatoes and carrots on top of the meat.

5. Cover lid securely; bring to high pressure for 17 minutes. Remove and allow pressure release of its own will.

6. Open the cooker once pressure has dropped and move the potatoes, meats and carrots to a serving dish. Cover and keep warm.

7. Skim the fat from the juices left in the pan. Uncover cooker and set over medium heat and simmer juices 5 minutes.

8. Whisk in the butter, if desired, 1 teaspoon at a time, Taste for seasoning and if required, add extra salt and pepper.

9. Let the gravy be at the table to pour over the meat.

Fajitas Steak

Serve this meat along with the thickened sauce over mashed potatoes or rice. Alternatively, you could serve the drained meat and veggies wrapped in a flour tortilla.

Servings: 4

Ingredients

1 pound round steak

2 cups frozen whole kernel corn, thawed

1 small green bell pepper, seeded and diced

1¼ cups tomato juice

½ teaspoon chili powder

1 small onion, peeled& diced

Salt and freshly ground black pepper, to taste

1 tablespoon cornstarch, optional

¼ cup cold water, optional

Preparation

1. Trim the fat from the meat and discard. Cut meat into ½-inch diced pieces and place in the pressure cooker.

2. Add the pepper, salt, chili powder, onion, bell pepper, corn and tomato juice. Lock lid into place, bring to low pressure and maintain this pressure for 12 minutes.

3. Remove from heat; allow pressure to release for 5 minutes naturally. Quick release any remaining pressure.

4. If you want to thicken the sauce, whisk the cornstarch and the cold water together in a small bowl. Bring the pressure cooker back to medium heat and then bring to a simmer. Next, whisk in the cornstarch slurry, cook uncovered for 5 minutes and add more salt & pepper if needed.

Dijon Pork Chops

Servings: 4

Ingredients

1 tablespoon margarine or butter

1/2 cup chicken broth

4 boneless pork chops, about 1-inch thick

1/4 cup white wine

1 teaspoon grated fresh ginger

2 tablespoons Dijon mustard

1 tablespoon cornstarch

2 green onions, sliced

1 tablespoon water

Preparation

1. Place the butter or margarine in the pressure cooker. Set to brown and let butter melt. Add the pork chops and brown meat on both sides evenly.

2. Meanwhile, add together the ginger, broth, mustard and wine. Once meat is browned, pour the broth mixture over the chops.

3. Cover lid and cook at high Pressure for 8 minutes. Quick- release pressure. Transfer chops to warm serving bowl. Add cornstarch and water, and stir to form a smooth paste.

4. Stir green onions and cornstarch mixture into drippings. Set to Brown and cook, stirring frequently until thickened. Spoon the sauce over chops.

Pressure Cooker Chicken Recipes

Chili –Ginger Chicken

Serve these chicken thighs and sauce with rice, topped with either coleslaw on a hamburger bun, or coleslaw rolled into flour tortillas with romaine leaves.

Servings: 6

<u>Ingredients</u>

3 pounds boneless, skinless chicken thighs

1 cup plain yogurt

2 teaspoons fresh ginger, grated

1 clove garlic, peeled & minced

¼ teaspoon cayenne pepper

4 tablespoons butter

8 teaspoons ketchup

1 14½-ounce can diced tomatoes

½ teaspoon chili powder

½ cup cashews, crushed

Salt& freshly ground black pepper, to taste

1 teaspoon sugar

Plain yogurt or sour cream, optional

2-3 drops red coloring, optional

<u>Preparation</u>

1. Combine the yogurt, cayenne pepper, ginger and garlic in a bowl. Add chicken thighs and marinate for at least 4 hours.

2. Remove chicken thighs from marinade and add to the pressure cooker together with the undrained chili powder, ketchup and diced tomatoes.

3. Lock the lid of the pressure cooker and bring to low pressure, maintaining pressure for 8 minutes. Quickly release the pressure.

4. Using a slotted spoon, move the cooked chicken thighs to a serving dish and keep warm.

5. Puree the tomatoes with an immersion blender. Whisk in the sugar and butter. Add the cashews and stir. Add salt and pepper, to taste.

6. If you prefer your sauce less spicy, stir in some sour cream or plain yogurt 1 tablespoon at a time until desired taste is attained.

7. If desired, add red food coloring. Pour over the chicken thighs and serve.

Chicken Bordeaux
Serve with cooked rice, buttered egg noodles or potatoes.

Servings: 6

<u>Ingredients</u>

4 ounces mushrooms, sliced

3 pounds chicken pieces

1 14½-ounce can diced tomatoes

3 tbsp vegetable oil

1 teaspoon cracked black pepper

1 clove garlic, peeled and crushed

1 cup dry white wine

<u>Preparation</u>

1. In the pressure cooker, bring oil to temperature over medium high heat and add garlic, sautéing to infuse the garlic flavor into the oil.

2. Now take out the garlic and discard.

3. Rub the chicken with pepper. In the pressure cooker, place the chicken pieces skin side down. Pour in the tomatoes and wine. Add the mushrooms.

4. Lock the lid and bring to low pressure for 10 minutes. Take out from the heat and quickly release pressure.

5. Transfer chicken to a serving platter and keep it warm. Return pressure cooker to heat and simmer sauce until it thickens. Pour over the chicken.

Satay-Rich Chicken

Serve over cooked jasmine rice. Sprinkle this chicken dish with the peanut sauce. Serve with Indian flatbread along with a cucumber salad.

Servings: 4

<u>Ingredients</u>

1 pound boneless, skinless chicken breasts, cut into bite-size pieces

½ cup coconut milk

2 teaspoons red curry paste

1 tablespoon fish sauce

1 teaspoon light brown sugar

¼ teaspoon freshly ground black pepper

½ teaspoon ground turmeric

<u>Preparations</u>

1. Add all the ingredients to the pressure cooker. Stir thoroughly. Lock the lid into place, bringing to low pressure. Maintain this pressure for 10 minutes.

2. Take out from heat and let the pressure release naturally.

3. Remove lid, return pan to medium heat and simmer until sauce is thickened. Pour over cooked jasmine rice.

Chicken Pesto Sauce

The pesto contains salt and pepper already so there's none in this recipe. However, have it on the table for diners who want to add more.

Servings: 4

<u>Ingredients</u>

1/3 cup pesto

3 pounds bone-in chicken thighs

1 large sweet onion, peeled and sliced

8 small red potatoes, peeled

½ cup chicken broth

1 1-pound bag baby carrots

<u>Preparations</u>

1. Remove skin and fat from the chicken thighs and then add to a large zip-closure bag together with the pesto. Seal bag and shake to coat the chicken in the pesto.

41

2. Now add the onions and broth to the pressure cooker. Place the cooking rack or trivet on top of the onions.

3. Place the chicken on the rack and add the carrots and potatoes to the top of the chicken.

4. Lock the lid into place. Bring it to high pressure and maintain this pressure for 11 minutes. Remove pressure cooker from the heat. Release the pressure quickly.

5. Remove the chicken, carrots and potatoes and place in a serving platter. Remove cooking rack or the trivet with tongs.

6. Remove any fat left from the juices in the pan. Strain the juices over the chicken and veggies. Serve hot.

Chicken & Dressing Sunday

Servings: 4-6

Ingredients

1 stalk celery, chopped

2 to 2-1/2 pounds bone-in chicken pieces

1 tablespoon margarine or butter

1 teaspoon paprika

1/2 cup chopped onion

1 teaspoon rubbed sage

4 cups herb-seasoned stuffing

2 tablespoons minced fresh parsley

1 teaspoon salt

1/2 teaspoon pepper

1 cup water

1/2 cup sliced mushrooms, optional

Preparations

1. Sprinkle the chicken with paprika and place butter in the pressure cooker. Set to Brown and leave to melt.

2. Add chicken in small quantities and brown on both sides evenly. Set browned chicken aside.

3. Stir celery, mushroom and onion into the butter left in the pressure cooker.

4. Next, Sauté for 3 minutes, stirring often. Stir sage, parsley, salt and pepper into vegetables.

5. Place the chicken over vegetables and add water. Cover and cook for 20 minutes on High Pressure. Quickly release pressure.

6. Lift chicken out of liquid using a slotted spoon, leaving vegetables and liquid in the pressure cooker.

7. Set chicken aside and keep it warm. Add the stuffing into liquid and stir. Cover and cook on Steam for 3 minutes.

8. Serve the dressing with chicken.

Hungarian Paprikash Chicken

Serve this simple recipe with buttered egg noodles.

Servings: 4

Ingredients

4 chicken breast halves

2 tablespoons vegetable oil or ghee

1 cup chicken broth

1 medium sweet onion, peeled & diced

1 tablespoon flour

5 cloves garlic, peeled & minced

1 green bell pepper, peeled & diced

2 tablespoons Hungarian paprika

¾ cup sour cream

¼ cup tomato sauce

Salt& freshly ground black pepper, to taste

Preparation

1. Bring the oil or ghee to temperature over medium-high heat in the pressure cooker. Add the green pepper and onion; sauté for 3 minutes. Add garlic and stir. Add the chicken pieces, placing skin side down; leave to brown.

2. Combine the chicken broth, tomato sauce and paprika. Pour over the chicken. Lock lid and bring to low pressure for 10 minutes.

3. Take out the pan from the heat, quick-release the pressure and then transfer the chicken to a platter. Keep warm. Return pan to heat.

4. First, stir the flour into sour cream and then stir into the pan juices. Cook, stir and simmer for 5 minutes. Add salt and pepper to taste. Pour sauce over chicken.

Balsamic Chicken & Onions

<u>Ingredients:</u>

1 ½ kilo Chicken Thighs

2 chicken cubes

2 cups of sweet onions, minced

2 cups carrots, chopped

1 cup raisins or mixed berries

6 garlic cloves or more

1 cup balsamic vinegar

2 bay leaves

1 cup red wine

<u>Preparations</u>

1. Place all ingredients in the pot. Add salt and pepper if you like.

2. Close pressure cooker lid and set it to airtight. Leave it on for 20 minutes and serve.

3. Enjoy with rice and mashed potatoes.

Spicy Chicken Salad

If the chicken is prepared the night before and refrigerated in its own broth, the chicken will be very moist.

Servings: 6

Ingredients

1 medium sweet onion, peeled &quartered

3 pounds chicken breast halves, bone-in and with skin

1 stalk celery, diced

1 large carrot, peeled & diced

8 peppercorns

1½ cups apples, diced

½ cup sour cream

1 cup slivered almonds, toasted

2 tablespoons red onion or shallot, diced

¼ cup mayonnaise

½ cup seedless green grapes, halved

1 cup celery, sliced

2–3 tablespoons curry powder

½ teaspoon of freshly ground black pepper

Salt, to taste

1 cup water

Preparations

1. Add the chicken, peppercorns, onion, celery, carrot and water to the pressure cooker.

2. Close lid and bring to high pressure, maintaining pressure for 10 minutes

3. Remove from heat; let the pressure release on its own for 10 minutes and then quick-release any pressure left.

4. With a slotted spoon, transfer chicken to bowl. Strain the broth that is in the pressure cooker and then pour it over the chicken. Leave the chicken in the broth to cool.

5. To make the salad, add the curry powder, sour cream, mayonnaise, pepper and salt pepper to a bowl. Stir well. Add the almonds, celery, apples, and shallot or red onion.

6. Remove chicken from the bones. Throw away the bones and skin. Now dice the chicken and fold them into the salad mixture. Refrigerate until ready to serve.

Chicken In Orange Sauce

Serve Chicken in Orange Sauce over rice. Have soy sauce available at the table.

Servings: 8

<u>Ingredients</u>

3 pounds boneless, skinless chicken thighs

1 1-pound bag baby carrots, quartered

2 tablespoons butter

1 teaspoon paprika

½ cup slivered almonds

1/8 teaspoon cinnamon

Pinch ground cloves

1/8 teaspoon ginger

½ cup white raisins

1½ cups orange juice

1 tablespoon cornstarch

¼ cup cold water

½ teaspoon salt

Preparations

1. In the pressure cooker, bring the butter to temperature over medium heat.

2.Now add the chicken thighs, fry on each side for 2 minutes and then add the ginger, paprika, cinnamon, raisins, cloves, orange juice, almonds, carrots and salt.

3. Lock lid, bring to low pressure for 10 minutes. Quickly release the pressure and remove the lid.

4. Add cornstarch and the water together and whisk into the sauce, stirring and cooking for 3 minutes or until the sauce thickened and the raw cornstarch taste is cooked.

East Indies Chicken

Serve with couscous or cooked rice and a cucumber salad. Make a tangy vinaigrette for the salad with equal parts rice vinegar and chili sauce, a little sesame oil, and sugar, garlic powder, salt, and pepper to taste.

Servings: 6

<u>Ingredients</u>

6 boneless, skinless chicken breasts

2 cloves garlic, peeled & minced

½ cup plain yogurt

2 teaspoons cornstarch

1 tablespoon lemon juice

¼ teaspoon salt

1 teaspoon paprika

1 teaspoon curry powder

¼ teaspoon freshly ground black pepper

2 teaspoons cold water

1 teaspoon turmeric

½ teaspoon ground ginger or 2 teaspoons grated fresh ginger

1 cup water

<u>Preparation</u>

1. In a bowl, Mix together water, lemon juice, yogurt, garlic, turmeric, ginger, curry powder, paprika, salt and pepper; add the chicken and then marinate for 1 hour at room temperature.

2. Pour the marinade and chicken into the pressure cooker. Lock the lid and bring to low pressure for 10 minutes.

3. Remove pressure cooker from heat and release the pressure quickly. Transfer chicken to a platter and keep warm.

4. Add the cornstarch to the cold water and mix, stirring into the yogurt mixture that is in the pressure cooker.

5. Return pressure cooker to heat and bring to a boil over medium-high heat. Let it boil for 3 minutes or until the mixture thickens. Pour the sauce over the chicken and serve immediately recipe.

Pressure Cooker Fish & Seafood Recipes

Creamy Crab

With the pressure cooker's moist environment, the flavors melds without drying the crabmeat out. Serve this tasty sauce over egg noodles, cooked rice, or toast together with a large tossed salad.

Servings: 4

<u>Ingredients</u>

1 pound uncooked lump crabmeat

½ cup heavy cream

4 tablespoons butter

¼ cup chicken broth

½ stalk celery, finely diced

Salt& freshly ground black pepper, to taste

1 small red onion, peeled & finely diced

<u>Preparation</u>

1. Melt the butter in the pressure cooker over medium heat. Add the celery; sauté until celery starts to soften. Add the onion; stir and sauté for 3 minutes.

2. Add the crabmeat and broth; stir. Secure lid and bring to low pressure for 3 minutes. Quickly release the pressure and take out the lid.

3. Stir in the cream carefully. Add salt and pepper as needed. Serve.

Catfish In French Sauce

Serve over cooked rice. Have hot sauce available at the table for those who want it.

Servings: 4

<u>Ingredients</u>

1½ pounds catfish fillets, rinse, pat dry & cut into bite-size pieces

2 teaspoons dried minced onion

1 14½-ounce can diced tomatoes

¼ teaspoon onion powder

¼ teaspoon garlic powder

1 teaspoon dried minced garlic

1 teaspoon hot paprika

1 medium green bell pepper, seeded & diced

¼ teaspoon dried tarragon

1 stalk celery, finely diced

Salt & freshly ground pepper, to taste

½ cup chili sauce

¼ teaspoon sugar

<u>Preparation</u>

1. Add all the ingredients except fish to the pressure cooker and mix well. Stir the fillets gently into the tomato mixture

2. Secure lid and bring the pressure cooker to low pressure for 5 minutes.

52

3. Quickly release the pressure. Take out the lid. Stir gently and add salt and pepper if needed.

Easy Paella
Servings: 6

<u>Ingredients</u>

2 tablespoons olive oil

1 onion, chopped

2 cloves garlic, minced

1/2 cup clam juice

1 pound chicken breast tenders

1/2 cup chopped red pepper

1/2 cup chopped green pepper

1/2 cup of chopped tomatoes

1 (5 ounce) package of yellow rice

1/2 teaspoon oregano leaves, dried

1/4 teaspoon pepper

3/4 cup chicken of broth

1/2 pound deveined shrimp, fresh shelled

1/2 cup frozen peas

<u>Preparation</u>

1. Pour the olive oil into the pressure cooker. Set it to Brown and leave oil to heat.

2. Add garlic, chicken and onion and sauté for 3 to 5 minutes.

3. Add red pepper, green pepper, yellow rice, oregano, tomatoes, chicken broth, clam juice and pepper.

4. Cover and cook for 8 minutes on High Pressure. Quick- release pressure. Stir in peas and shrimp and peas. Cover and cook for 2 minutes on low pressure.

Red Miso Snapper

Servings: 4

Ingredients

2 pounds red snapper fillets

1 tablespoon red miso paste

1 tablespoon rice wine

1 2-inch piece fresh ginger, peeled & cut into 1 inch long matchsticks

4 green onions, halve lengthwise & cut into 2-inchlong pieces

2 teaspoons sesame oil

2 teaspoons fermented black beans

1 teaspoon dark soy sauce

2 cloves garlic, peeled and minced

½ teaspoon Asian chili paste

Salt

Water

Preparation

1. (Insert the rack in the pressure cooker. Get a glass pie pan that can fit on the rack in the pressure cooker and pour enough water into it till it fills just below the top of the rack).

2. Mix the miso, black beans, rice wine, sesame oil, chili paste and soy sauce in a small bowl. Sprinkle a little salt over the fish fillets and rub with the miso mixture on both sides.

3. Place half of the peeled and cut ginger on the bottom of a glass pie plate. Sprinkle half of the garlic over the ginger.

4. Place half of the cut green onions over the garlic and ginger. Place the fish fillets in the pie plate and then sprinkle the ginger, onions and garlic over the top. Place the pie plate properly on the rack inside the pressure cooker.

5. Close lid and bring to high pressure for 3 minutes. Take out from heat and quickly release the pressure. Serve.

Fish Steaks With Olive Sauce And Tomato

Servings: 2

Ingredients

2 firm fish steaks, cut 1-inch thick

2/3 cup sliced mushrooms

2 tablespoons olive oil

2 cloves garlic, minced

1/2 cup chopped onion

4 Roma tomatoes, chopped

2 tablespoons capers, drained

1/4 cup chopped, pitted kalamata olives

2 tablespoons minced fresh parsley

1/8 teaspoon dried crushed red pepper

1/4 teaspoon salt

1/4 cup white wine

Preparation

1. Pour olive oil into the pressure cooker. Set it to Brown and let the oil heat. Add garlic and onion and sauté for 2 to 3 minutes.

2. Add remaining ingredients, except fish and stir. Cover and cook at High Pressure for 5 minutes. Release pressure quickly.

3. Place fish in sauce, spoon some sauce up over fish. Set it to Steam, cover and cook for 5 minutes.

Calamari In Tomato Stew

The dried herbs may be omitted if you have basil and fresh parsley. Simply stir 1 tablespoon of each of them into the calamari after quick-releasing the pressure.

Servings: 4

Ingredients

2½ pounds calamari

2 tablespoons olive oil

1 small stalk celery, finely diced

1 small white onion, peeled & diced

1 small carrot, peeled& grated

3 cloves garlic, peeled& minced

1 28-ounce can diced tomatoes

1 teaspoon dried parsley

1 teaspoon dried basil

Salt & freshly ground black pepper, to taste

½ cup white wine

1/3 cup water

Preparation

1. In the pressure cooker, bring the oil to temperature. Add the celery and carrots; sauté for 2 minutes.

2. Stir in the onions; sauté for 3 minutes. Stir in the garlic and then sauté it 30 seconds.

3. Clean, wash the calamari and pat dry. Add to the pressure cooker together with the remaining ingredients.

4. Secure lid into place and bring to low pressure for 10 minutes. Quickly release pressure. Serve.

Shrimp Chicken Jambalaya

Servings: 4 to 6

Ingredients

12 ounces large shrimp, peeled & deveined

2 skinless, boneless, chicken breast halves, cut into 1/2-inch cubes

1 cup converted rice, uncooked

1 onion, chopped

1 large green pepper, diced

3 stalks celery, sliced

2 cloves garlic, minced

1 can (8 ounces) tomato sauce

1 tablespoon vegetable oil

1-1/4 cups chicken broth

1/2 teaspoon dried thyme leaves

1/2 teaspoon salt

1 bay leaf

1/2 teaspoon white pepper

1/4 teaspoon cayenne pepper

2 dashes hot pepper sauce

1/2 teaspoon sage

Preparation

1. Pour vegetable oil into the pressure cooker. Set it to Brown and let it heat. Add onion, chicken, garlic green pepper and celery.

2. Sauté until the vegetables are just tender. Add the remaining ingredients, cover and cook at High Pressure for 9 minutes. Quick- release pressure.

Orange Roughy With Black Olive Sauce

Servings: 2

Ingredients

2 (8-ounce, 1-inch-thick) orange roughy fillets

3 tablespoons butter, melted

4 teaspoons freshly squeezed lime juice

6 sprigs fresh dill or¼ teaspoon dried dill

6 Kalamata or black olives, pitted and chopped

3/8 cup dry white wine

4 thin slices white onion

3/8 cup water

Sea salt, to taste

Preparation

1. Pour the water and wine into the pressure cooker. Place the trivet in the cooker. Wash the fish and pat dry. Sprinkle with a little salt.

2. Place 2 onion slices on the trivet and top with a sprig of dill each. Place fish over the dill and onion and put 1 sprig of dill on each. Top with the remaining 2 onion slices.

3. Close lid and bring to high pressure for 5 minutes. Take out from heat to allow the pressure to release on its own for 5 minutes. Quick-release any pressure that is left.

4. To make the sauce, whisk lime juice, butter and ½ tablespoon of cooking liquid from the fish; add the olives and stir. Garnish with the remaining dill.

Low Town Shrimp Boil

Servings: 6

<u>Ingredient</u>

1/2 pound smoked sausage, cut into 1/2-inch slices

1 pound large fresh shrimp, in shells

1 can (14.5 ounces) chicken broth

1/3 cup white wine

1/4 teaspoon dried crushed red pepper

4 whole black peppercorns

1 bay leaf

5 to 6 whole new red potatoes

2 ears corn, cut into thirds

3/4 cup water

<u>Preparation</u>

1. Place wine, broth, corn, water, bay leaf, peppercorns, red potatoes and crushed red pepper in the pressure cooker. Secure lid into place and cook at High Pressure for 4 minutes. Quick- release pressure.

2. Stir in shrimp sausage. Cover and cook at Low Pressure for 2 minutes. Release pressure quickly.

Country Grouper

Servings: 4

<u>Ingredients</u>

2 tablespoons vegetable or peanut oil

4 grouper fillets

1 small onion, peeled & diced

1 tablespoon tomato paste

1 green bell pepper, seeded and diced

1 stalk celery, diced

1 14½-ounce can diced tomatoes

1 teaspoon sugar

Pinch basil

¼ cup water

½ teaspoon chili powder

Salt & pepper, to taste

<u>Preparation</u>

1. In the pressure cooker, bring the oil to temperature over medium-high heat. Add the green pepper, onion and celery; sauté for 3 minutes.

2. Stir in tomato paste, undrained tomatoes, water, basil, sugar and chili powder.

61

3. Rinse fish, pat dry and cut into bite-size pieces. Add salt and pepper, to taste. Stir the fish pieces gently into the sauce in the pressure cooker.

4. Secure lid and bring to high pressure for 5 minutes. Quickly release the pressure.

Pressure Cooker Turkey Recipes

Zesty Turkey Ratatouille

Serve this tasty dish over cooked potatoes or pasta or with thick slices of French bread, buttered.

Servings: 4

Ingredients

1 pound boneless, skinless, turkey breast

¼ teaspoon dried red pepper flakes

2 medium zucchini, thickly sliced

2 tablespoons olive or vegetable oil

1 medium sweet onion, peeled and diced

½ pound mushrooms, sliced

1 medium eggplant, peeled and diced

1 medium green bell pepper, seeded and diced

1 28-ounce can diced tomatoes

2 cloves garlic, peeled and minced

3 tablespoons tomato paste

2 teaspoons dried basil

Parmigiano-Reggiano cheese, grated

Salt and freshly ground black pepper, to taste

Ingredients

1. Begin by cutting the turkey into bite-size pieces and then bring the oil to temperature over medium heat. Next, add the turkey; fry until it begins to brown.

2. Add the eggplant, zucchini, onion, mushrooms, bell pepper, tomato paste, red pepper flakes, undrained diced tomatoes, basil and garlic.

3. Secure lid and bring to low pressure for 5 minutes. Remove heat and quick-release pressure.

4. Add salt and pepper, to taste.

Leftover Turkey Chili

Use up your Thanksgiving leftovers by making this dish Serve with cornbread or serve as a topper for baked potatoes & a tossed salad.

Servings: 8

Ingredients

¼ cup chicken broth

3 pounds lean ground turkey

2 tablespoons extra virgin olive oil

1 large red bell pepper, seeded and diced

2 large sweet onions, peeled and diced

4 cloves garlic, peeled and minced

1½ teaspoons ground cumin

3 tablespoons chili powder

1 teaspoon ground allspice

1 teaspoon ground coriander

1 teaspoon ground cinnamon

1 teaspoon dried oregano

2 14½-ounce cans diced tomatoes

2 tablespoons cornmeal

1 bay leaf

Salt and freshly ground black pepper, to taste

<u>Preparation</u>

1. In the pressure cooker, bring the oil to temperature over medium-high heat. Add the turkey frying for 5 minutes and occasionally, using a spatula to break it apart.

2. Stir in the bell pepper and onion; stir-fry together with the meat for 3 minutes then stir in the chili powder, garlic, cumin, cinnamon, allspice, oregano and coriander.

3. Sauté the spices along with the meat for 2 minutes. Add the undrained tomatoes, bay leaf and broth.

4. Close lid and bring to high pressure for 10 minutes. Remove from heat and allow natural release of pressure. Remove the lid.

5. Take the pressure cooker back to the heat. Add the cornmeal, stir and simmer until the cornmeal thickens the chili. Discard the bay leaf. Add salt and pepper to taste.

<u>Cincinnati-Style Turkey Chili</u>

1. When you add the other spices, stir in1 teaspoon of cinnamon.

2. After simmering the chili and cornmeal together, add 2 tablespoons of semisweet chocolate chips and stir. Keep simmering the chili until the chocolate is fully melted.

3. Serve this chili over cooked spaghetti and top it with grated Cheddar cheese.

Yogurt Sauced Turkey Breast

Serve this mouth-watering meal over couscous or cooked rice with a cucumber-yogurt salad. To make cucumber-yogurt salad, add together plain yogurt, mint, salt, ginger and garlic. Spritz with lemon juice and add cucumbers, thinly sliced.

Servings: 6

Ingredients

1 teaspoon ground turmeric

1 cup plain yogurt

1 teaspoon yellow mustard seeds

1 teaspoon ground cumin

1 pound boneless turkey breast

1 1-pound bag baby peas and pearl onions

1 tablespoon ghee or butter

½teaspoon freshly ground black pepper

¼ teaspoon salt

Preparation

1. Combine the yogurt, cumin, turmeric, mustard seeds, pepper and salt in a large bowl. Cut the turkey into pieces.

2. Add the yogurt mixture to the cut turkey. Cover in the refrigerator to marinate for 4 hrs.

3. Melt the butter or ghee in the pressure cooker. Add the turkey pieces and yogurt mixture.

4. Close lid and bring to low pressure for 8 minutes. Remove and allow pressure release for 5 minutes naturally. Quick-release any pressure that is left.

5. Remove the lid and stir in the pearl onions and peas. Return the pan to medium heat.

6. Simmer until the veggies are cooked and the sauce is thickened. Serve.

Turkey à la Majestic

Enjoy this almost full meal made of meat, veggies and sauce.

Servings: 4

Ingredients

¼ cup all-purpose flour

1 pound skinless, boneless turkey breast

3 tablespoons butter or ghee

1 small sweet onion, peeled and diced

1 4-ounce can mushrooms, sliced& drained

1 cup frozen peas

1 14-ounce can chicken broth

1 2-ounce jar pimientos, drained and diced

½ cup heavy cream

½ cup milk, optional

Salt and freshly ground black pepper, to taste

Preparation

1. In the pressure cooker, bring the butter or ghee to temperature over medium heat. Next, cut the turkey into bite-size pieces and add them to the pressure cooker. Add onion as well.

2. Stir-fry for 5 minutes then stir in the mushrooms, peas, broth and pimientos. Close lid and bring to low pressure for 6 minutes. Remove and allow pressure to release on its own.

3. Remove the lid, return the pressure cooker to medium heat and add the flour to the cream, whisking in. When the pan juices reach a low boil, add the flour-cream mixture, whisking in.

4. Stir and cook until the flour taste is cooked out and the mixture thickens. If it gets too thick, add the optional milk until it gets it to the desired consistency. Add salt and pepper to taste.

Turkey Drumsticks& Veggiee Soup

The turkey drumsticks must fit into your pressure cooker so measure before you begin. The end of the bone may touch the lid of the pressure cooker as long as it does not block the vent.

Servings: 6

Ingredients

2 1¼-pound turkey drumsticks, skin removed

6 medium potatoes, peeled and cut into quarters

1 10-ounce package frozen green beans, thawed

1 tablespoon extra virgin olive oil

2 14½-ounce cans diced tomatoes

1 clove garlic, peeled and minced

6 large carrots, peeled and sliced

12 small onions, peeled

½ ounce dried mushrooms

2 stalks celery, finely diced

¼ teaspoon dried oregano

1 bay leaf

1 10-ounce package frozen baby peas, thawed

¼ teaspoon dried rosemary

2 strips orange zest

1 10-ounce package frozen whole kernel corn, thawed

Fresh parsley or cilantro

Salt and freshly ground black pepper, to taste

Preparation

1. Add the olive oil to the pressure cooker and then bring to temperature over medium heat. Next, add the garlic, sautéing for 10 seconds.

2. Stir in the potatoes, tomatoes, carrots, celery, bay leaf, onions, mushrooms, rosemary, orange zest, oregano, salt and pepper. Place the 2 drumsticks side down in the pan.

3. Cover and bring to high pressure for 12 minutes. Remove and allow the pressure to drop on its own accord and then quick-release any remaining pressure.

4. Remove the drumsticks, trim the meat from the bone and cut into bite-size pieces then return the meat to the pot

5. Add the peas, corn, green beans; cook over medium heat for 5 minutes. Remove bay leaf and orange zest; discard. Add salt and pepper to taste.

Mini Turkey Loaves

Enjoy hot or cold in sandwiches or serve with mashed potatoes and vegetables.

Servings: 6

Ingredients

½ teaspoon dried basil

1½ pounds lean ground turkey

1 medium carrot, peeled and grated

1 small onion, peeled and diced

½ cup butter cracker crumbs

1 tablespoon light brown sugar, optional

1 small stalk celery, minced

1 clove garlic, peeled and minced

1 tablespoon mayonnaise

¼ teaspoon freshly ground black pepper

¼ teaspoon salt

3 tablespoons ketchup

1 large egg

Preparation

1. In a large bowl, mix all the ingredients together. Divide the mixture between 2 mini bread loaf pans and pack them down into the pans.

2. Next, add the rack to the pressure cooker and pour hot water into the cooker to get to the level rack top. Place the pans on the rack.

3. Secure lid and bring to low pressure for 20 minutes. Remove from heat and let the pressure release naturally. Take out the lid. Transfer to a serving platter or serve directly from the pans.

File Turkey Gumbo

To enjoy a more robust flavor, add cayenne pepper with the black pepper or place hot sauce at the table.

Servings: 4

Ingredients

½ pound smoked Andouille sausage or kielbasa

2 tablespoons vegetable or olive oil

1 pound boneless, skinless turkey breast

4 cloves garlic, peeled and minced

1 large sweet onion, peeled and diced

1½ teaspoons dried thyme

1 teaspoon filé powder (adds flavor and thickens the gumbo)

½teaspoon freshly ground black pepper

¼ teaspoon dried red pepper flakes

¼ teaspoon dried sage

3 bay leaves

½ cup white wine

2 stalks celery, sliced

1 10-ounce package frozen sliced okra, thawed

1 large green bell pepper, seeded and diced

½ cup fresh cilantro, minced

1 14-ounce can chicken broth

1 14½-ounce can diced tomatoes

Preparation

1. In the pressure cooker, bring the oil to temperature over medium heat and add the sausage slices.

2. Next, cut the turkey into pieces and add them to the pressure cooker. Add the onion, stir-frying for 3 minutes.

3. Stir in the red pepper flakes, garlic, filé powder, thyme, sage and black pepper and sauté for 1 minute.

4. Deglaze the pan with the wine, scraping the pressure cooker bottom to loosen anything that may be stuck to the bottom of the pan. Add the remaining ingredients and stir.

5. Close lid and bring to low pressure for 8 minutes. Remove from heat and let the pressure release on its own.

6. Remove lid. Remove bay leaves and discard. Add more seasoning if necessary.

Lemony Turkey Tenderloins

Servings: 4

<u>Ingredients</u>

1-3/4 to 2 pounds turkey breast tenderloins, sliced 1/2-inch

2 tablespoons margarine or butter

Fresh minced parsley

3 tablespoons lemon juice

1/3 cup plus 1 tablespoon water, divided

2 cloves garlic, minced

1 tablespoon cornstarch

1 teaspoon salt

1/2 teaspoon pepper

<u>Preparation</u>

1. Place the butter in the pressure cooker and set to Brown. Once the butter melts, add turkey slices, in small quantities, and brown on both sides evenly. Season with garlic salt and pepper.

2. Mix 1/3 cup water and lemon juice together and pour over turkey. Close lid and cook at High Pressure for12 minutes. Quick- release pressure.

3. Transfer turkey to warm serving plate. Combine the cornstarch and 1 tablespoon of the water left and stir to form a smooth paste. Add the cornstarch mixture into the drippings and stir.

3. Set to Brown, cook and stir for1- 2 minutes or until it thickened. Spoon the sauce over turkey. Sprinkle with parsley

Pressure Cooker Soups

Scotchy Broths
More like a soup than a broth. Enjoy it!

Servings: 4

Ingredients

4 lamb shoulder chops

2 leeks, white part only

2 medium potatoes, peeled & diced

1 large carrot, peeled and diced

1/3 cup pearl barley

1 stalk celery, thinly sliced

Fresh parsley, minced, optional

Salt &freshly ground black pepper, to taste

6 cups water

Preparation:

1. Dice the leeks (white part only), rinse thoroughly and drain. Add the diced leeks to the pressure cooker and then add the lamb chops, carrot, barley celery, potatoes, salt, pepper and water.

2. Seal the lid and bring to high pressure for 9 minutes. Take out from the heat and quickly release the pressure. Remove lid. Taste and add extra salt and pepper if necessary.

3. Transfer 1 lamb chop to each of 4 bowls. Ladle the soup over the meat. If desired, garnish with parsley.

Chicken With Rice Soup

Servings: 6

Ingredients

1/3 cup uncooked, long-grain rice

1-112 cups diced, cooked chicken

5 cups chicken stock

1/4 cup diced carrot

1/4 cup diced onion

1/4 cup diced celery

1 teaspoon salt

1/4 teaspoon pepper

Preparation:

1. Place the ingredients in the pressure cooker. Close lid and cook at High Pressure for 5 minutes. Gradually release pressure.

Portuguese Kale Soup

Collard greens can be used instead of kale, but this will change the flavor a bit.

Servings: 6

Ingredients

2 15-ounce cans cannellini beans, rinsed & drained

4 cups chicken broth

4 large potatoes, peeled &diced

1 pound kale

1 tablespoon extra virgin olive oil

½ pound linguica or kielbasa, sliced

1 large yellow onion, peeled & thinly sliced

Salt and freshly ground black pepper, to taste

Preparation:

1. Trim the ribs from the kale and slice thinly into strips. Pour cold water into a bowl and soak the kale inside it for 1 hour then drain well.

2. Add the oil, kielbasa or linguica and onions to the pressure cooker and stir well. Place over medium heat and sauté until the onions are soft.

3. Add the drained kale, potatoes, broth, chicken and beans. Cover and bring to low pressure for 8 minutes.

4. Remove from heat and let pressure release for 5 minutes naturally. Quick-release any remaining pressure. Remove the lid. Add salt and pepper to taste.

Protein- Rich Lentil Soup

Instead of stirring the spinach into the soup, you could double the quantity and serve the soup with spinach salad.

Servings: 6

<u>Ingredients</u>

5 cups chicken broth

1 cup dried brown lentils, rinsed and drained

1 tablespoon olive oil

2 cloves of garlic, peeled and minced

1 large carrot, peeled and diced

1 celery stalk, diced

1 large yellow onion, peeled and diced

3/8 cup Parmigiano-Reggiano cheese, grated

Salt and freshly ground black pepper, to taste

3 cups baby spinach, washed and dried, optional

<u>Preparation</u>

1. In the pressure cooker, bring the oil to temperature over medium heat. Add the carrot and celery and sauté 2 minutes.

2. Add the onion and sauté until the onion is transparent. Next, add the garlic, sautéing for 30 seconds.

3. Stir in the broth and lentils. Lock the lid and bring to high pressure for 8 minutes. Remove from heat and let the pressure release of its own will. Remove the lid. If using spinach, stir it into the soup.

4. Bring back the pressure cooker to medium heat and cook until the spinach is wilted.

5. Season with salt and pepper. Serve and top each bowls with1 tablespoon of grated Parmigiano-Reggiano cheese.

Sizzling And Sour Soup
Servings: 4 to 6

<u>Ingredients</u>

1 can (10-1/2 ounces) chicken broth

2 cans (10-1/2 ounces each) beef broth

1 tablespoon sesame oil

1 package (8 ounces) sliced mushrooms

1 pound pork cutlets, cut into 1/4 x 2-inch slices

8 green onions, sliced

1 can (8 ounces) bamboo shoots, drained

1/4 to 1/2 teaspoon dried crushed red pepper

1/4 cup cornstarch

1/4 cup soy sauce

2 tablespoons cider vinegar

<u>Preparations</u>

1. Place the oil in the pressure cooker and set to Brown. Allow oil to heat and then add pork and brown on all sides. Add mushrooms and green onions and sauté for 3 to 5 minutes.

2. Add beef broth, dried crushed pepper, bamboo shoots, and chicken broth. Secure lid and cook on High Pressure for 5 minutes. Gradually Release pressure.

3. Combine cornstarch and soy sauce and blend thoroughly. Stir the cornstarch mixture into soup. Set it to Brown; cook, uncovered and stir frequently until thickened. Add the vinegar and stir.

Beef-Veggie Soup

Make Beef-Veggie Soup a tomato-based hearty dish by substituting two 15-ounce cans diced tomatoes for the beef broth.

Servings: 8

Ingredients

1 3-pound chuck roast

1 10-ounce package frozen whole kernel corn, thawed

4 cups beef broth

7 large carrots

1 large sweet onion, peeled and diced

2 stalks celery, finely diced

8 ounces fresh mushrooms, cleaned and sliced

1 teaspoon butter, melted

¼ teaspoon dried rosemary

1 tablespoon extra virgin olive oil

1 clove garlic, peeled and minced

1 tablespoon dried parsley

1 10-ounce package frozen baby peas, thawed

6 medium potatoes, peeled and diced

¼ teaspoon dried oregano

1 bay leaf

1 10-ounce package frozen green beans, thawed

Salt and freshly ground black pepper, to taste

<u>Tasty Substitutions:</u>

1. To add more flavor to this soup, substitute several strips of bite-size pieces of bacon for the oil. The bacon bits will be absorbed into the dish and offer extra crunch and zing.

2. Alternatively, use canned French onion soup instead of some of the beef broth.

<u>Preparation</u>

1. Peel the carrots, dice 6 of it and grate 1. Add the grated carrot, onion, celery, mushrooms, butter and oil to the pressure cooker.

2. Coat the vegetables in the oil and butter by stirring. Lock the lid and bring to low pressure for 1 minute. Quickly release the pressure and take out the lid.

3. Stir the garlic in. Add the diced carrots, broth, parsley, oregano, potatoes, bay leaf, rosemary, pepper and salt.

4. Trim the roast of fat and cut it into bite-size piece. Now add it to the pressure cooker and the vegetables as well, stir.

5. Close lid and bring to high pressure for 15 minutes. Quickly release the pressure and remove the lid.

6. Remove the bay leaf and discard. Stir in the peas, green beans and corn; cook for 5 minutes. Taste for seasoning

Caribbean Black Bean Soup

Like almost any bean dish, diced celery and carrot slices may be added to this soup once the onion is added.

Servings: 8

<u>Ingredients</u>

8 ounces smoked sausage

3 cloves garlic, peeled & minced

½ pound bacon, chopped

1 large yellow onion, peeled & diced

1 green bell pepper, seeded & diced

2 teaspoons paprika

½ teaspoon ground cumin

1 tablespoon red wine vinegar

½ teaspoon chili powder

¼ teaspoon coriander

1 bay leaf

6 cups chicken broth or water

1 smoked turkey wing or smoked ham hock

1 pound dried black beans, soaked overnight, rinsed &drained

1/8 teaspoon dried red pepper flakes or cayenne pepper

½ cup dry sherry

Salt and freshly ground black pepper, to taste

Preparation

1. Place bacon in the pressure cooker and fry over medium-high heat. Once the bacon starts to render its fat, lower the heat to medium and add the green pepper, sautéing for 3 minutes.

2. Add the onion and stir. Dice or slice the smoked sausage and stir into the onion, sautéing until the onion is tender.

3. Add the garlic, stir and add the cumin, coriander, bay leaf, paprika, chili powder, water or broth, beans and turkey wing or ham hock. Cover and bring to high pressure for 30 minutes.

4. Remove from the heat. Allow pressure to release on its own, leaving the lid in place for 20 minutes or more. Remove the lid.

5. Remove the turkey wing or ham hock and take the meat off of the bones; bring back meat to the pot. Remove bay leaf and discard.

6. Partially puree with a potato masher or immersion blender. Return the uncovered pan to medium heat. Bring to a simmer.

7. Stir in the dried red pepper flakes or cayenne pepper, vinegar and sherry. Simmer for 20 minutes. Taste for seasoning; add salt and pepper as needed. If desired, adjust the chili powder, herbs and red pepper flakes or cayenne pepper.

Sweet Potato Soup& Spiced Pear

Servings: 8

Ingredients

4 ripe pears, - peeled, cored and diced

1 tbsp vegetable oil

750g sweet potato, peeled and chopped

1 onion, chopped

6 cups chicken or vegetable stock

1 cloves garlic, chopped

1 tsp chili flakes

1 tbsp Ras El Hanout (Moroccan spice mix)

1 mustard cress to garnish, optional

Preparation

1. Preheat pressure Cooker for 2 minutes over medium heat. Add onion and oil and cook, stirring until the onion softens

2. Add Ras El Hanout, garlic, brown sugar and chili flakes. Cook and stir for 30 seconds. Add sweet potato, stock and pears, bringing to a boil.

3. Lower heat and simmer, covered, until the pears and sweet potato are tender.

4. Pour into a blender and blend for 10 seconds or mash until smooth. Serve garnished with cress.

Fresh Vine-Ripened Tomato Soup

Enjoy the summery taste of fresh vine-ripened tomatoes celebrated in this soup. Herbs and sautéed onion or shallots may be added. Consider your dietary needs when choosing the dairy product you want added to the soup. Also consider how rich you like your soup!

Servings: 4

Ingredients

½ teaspoon baking soda

8 medium fresh tomatoes

2 cups milk, heavy cream or half-and-half

1 cup water

Freshly ground black pepper, to taste

¼ teaspoon sea salt

Preparation

1. Wash the tomatoes then peel, seed, and dice them. Add them along with the tomato juice to the pressure cooker. Add water and salt.

2. Cover and place the pressure cooker over medium heat. Bring cooker to low pressure and maintain this pressure for 2 minutes. Quickly release the pressure and take out the lid.

3. Add the baking soda to the tomato mixture, stirring as you do. Once it's stopped foaming and bubbling, stir in the milk, heavy cream or half-and-half.

4. Cook until the soup is brought to temperature.

Hearty Split Pea Soup

Refrigerating this soup overnight makes it even tastier. Simply heat it up the next day and serve. It's also hearty enough to stand as the main dish alone. Serve with crusty bread.

Servings: 6

<u>Ingredients</u>

4 cups chicken broth

1 large sweet onion, peeled & diced

4 strips bacon, diced

2 large potatoes, peeled &diced

1 cup dried green split peas, rinsed

2 large carrots, peeled & sliced

2 smoked ham hocks

1 10-ounce package frozen peas, thawed, optional

Salt & freshly ground black pepper, to taste

<u>Preparation</u>

1. Place the bacon in pressure cooker and fry over medium heat until it begins to render its fat. Now, add the onion and sauté until soft.

2. Add the diced potatoes; stir and sauté for 3 minutes. Add the split peas, carrots, ham hocks and broth. Close lid and bring to low pressure for 15 minutes. Remove and let the pressure release naturally.

3. Remove lid. Remove the ham hocks with slotted spoon and leave to cool until the meat can easily be removed from the bones.

4. Taste the split peas and if they aren't cooked through, secure the lid back into place and cook at low pressure for 5 more minutes; remove from heat and release the pressure quickly.

5. If the split peas are cooked through, stir in the ham taken from the hocks into the soup. Alternatively, puree the soup with an immersion blender.

6. Bring back the soup to medium heat and then bring to a simmer. Stir in the peas if desired, and cook until they are heated. Add salt and pepper if needed.

Mediterranean Meatball Soup
Serve the soup topped with some feta cheese and with crusty bread.

Servings: 6

Ingredients

1 cup baby carrots, each sliced into thirds

6 tablespoons converted long-grain white rice, uncooked

6 cups chicken or vegetable broth or water

¼ pound ground pork

1 pound lean ground beef

1 clove garlic, peeled & minced

2 large potatoes, peeled and cut into cubes

1 small onion, peeled &minced

1 tablespoon dried parsley

2 teaspoons dried dill or mint

1 teaspoon dried oregano

Salt and freshly ground black pepper, to taste

3 large eggs

1 medium onion, peeled and chopped

1 stalk celery, finely chopped

2 tablespoons masa harina (corn flour)

1/3 cup fresh lemon juice

Preparation

1. Mix the meat, garlic, onion, rice, parsley, oregano, dill or mint, pepper, salt, and 1 egg in a large bowl. Shape into tiny meatballs and set aside.

2. Add 2 cups of water or broth to the pressure cooker. Add the meatballs, carrots, onion, celery and potatoes and then pour in the remaining water or broth to cover the vegetables and meatballs.

3. Lock the lid and bring to low pressure for 10 minutes. Remove from heat and allow the pressure to release naturally. Remove lid. Transfer the meatballs with a slotted spoon to a soup tureen; cover it and keep warm.

4. Return pan to medium heat and bring to a simmer. Beat the two remaining egg in a small bowl and whisk in the corn flour. Whisk in the lemon juice gradually.

5. Slowly ladle in 1 cup of the hot broth from the pressure cooker, beating constantly until the entire hot liquid has been incorporated into the corn flour- egg mixture.

6. Stir mixture into the pressure cooker. Next, stir and simmer until mixture is thickened. Add more seasonings if necessary. Pour over the meatballs and serve.

Barley- Mushroom Soup

Enjoy this vegetarian soup. Substitute beef or chicken broth for the water if you want it to complement a meat entrée.

Servings: 6

Ingredients

1 large carrot, peeled and diced

1 large sweet onion, peeled, halved, and sliced

2 tablespoons butter

½ cup pearl barley

2 stalks celery, diced

1 tablespoon olive or vegetable oil

2 cloves garlic, peeled and minced

8 ounces fresh mushrooms, cleaned and sliced

1 portobello mushroom cap, diced

1 bay leaf

6 cups water

2 tablespoons brandy or vermouth, optional

Salt & freshly ground black pepper, to taste

Preparation

1. Melt the butter in the pressure cooker and bring the oil to temperature over medium heat. Add the carrot and the celery; sauté 2 minutes. Add the onion and sauté until it is soft and transparent.

2. Next, stir in the mushrooms and garlic; sauté for 5 minutes. Once the onion begins to turn golden and the mushrooms release their moisture, stir in the barley, bay leaf water, and vermouth or brandy if using.

3. Lock the lid into place; bring to high pressure for 20 minutes. Take out from the heat and allow the pressure to release on its own. Remove the lid.

4. Take out the bay leaf and discard. Add salt and pepper to taste. Serve.

Pressure Cooker Stews And Chowders

Tex-Mex SouthWestern Stew

A blend of the southwestern flavors of Texas and Mexico, this hearty Tex-Mex Stew is best served over rice together with an avocado salad and baked corn chips or cornbread.

Servings: 8

Ingredients

1 7-ounce can green chilies

1 3½-pound English or chuck roast

2 14½-ounce cans diced tomatoes

2 tablespoons olive or vegetable oil

1 8-ounce can tomato sauce

1 green bell pepper, seeded and diced

1 large sweet onion, peeled and diced

6 cloves garlic, peeled and minced

1 teaspoon freshly ground black pepper

1 bunch fresh cilantro, chopped

1 tablespoon ground cumin

Cayenne pepper, to taste

2 tablespoons lime juice

2 jalapeño peppers, seeded & diced

Beef broth or water, optional

Preparation

1. Trim fat from roast and cut meat into 1 inch cubes. Add the vegetable or olive oil to the pressure cooker and bring to temperature over medium-high heat.

2. Next, add the beef, stir-frying until well browned. Stir in the tomatoes, chilies, onion, tomato sauce, garlic, bell pepper, black pepper, lime juice, cumin, jalapeño peppers and cayenne.

3. Add enough water or beef broth if needed, to cover the ingredients in the cooker. (Do not fill the cooker more than two-thirds full).

4. Secure lid and bring to low pressure for 1 hour. Take out from heat and let the pressure release naturally. Remove the lid. Add the cilantro and serve immediately

Simplified Chicken Stew

Serve with buttermilk biscuits or buttered dinner rolls.

Servings: 4

Ingredients

2 cups chicken broth

1 stalk celery, finely diced

1 cup baby carrots, cut in half

1 large onion, peeled and diced

1 tsp Mrs. Dash Garlic & Herb or Original Seasoning Blend

4 bone-in chicken breast halves

4 large potatoes, peeled and diced

2 tablespoons extra virgin olive oil

Salt and freshly ground black pepper, to taste

Preparation

1. Put the onions, celery, carrots, seasoning blend, oil and potatoes in a pressure cooker. Add broth.

2. Take out the skin from the chicken and discard it. Nestle the chicken pieces side down on top of the vegetables.

3. Lock the lid. Bring to high pressure and maintain pressure for 10 minutes.

4. Take it out from heat and release the pressure quickly. Remove the lid, stir, and season to taste.

Nippy Beef Stew

To enjoy an easy whole comfort food meal, serve with crackers or dinner rolls.

Servings: 8

Ingredients

1 10¾-ounce can condensed tomato soup

2 cups cooked roast beef, cut into bite-size pieces

1 10-ounce box frozen mixed vegetables

1 10½-ounce can condensed French onion soup

1 tablespoon Worcestershire sauce

1 tablespoon butter

1 24-ounce bag frozen vegetables

1 tablespoon all-purpose flour

Salt & freshly ground black pepper, to taste

2 cups water

<u>Preparation</u>

1. Add the soups, roast beef, Worcestershire sauce, frozen vegetables and water to the pressure cooker.

2. Cover lid and bring to low pressure for 3 minutes. Remove from heat, quickly release pressure and remove lid.

3. Make a paste by mixing the butter and flour in a small bowl. Ladle ½ cup of the soup broth into the bowl, whisk into the paste and then pour it into the stew.

4. Bring the stew to a boil by placing the uncovered pressure cooker over medium-high heat.

5. Boil for 2 minutes, stirring from time to time. Reduce heat and simmer for 2 minutes more.

Herbed Chicken Stew with Dumplings
To stretch this meal to 6 or 8 main dish servings, serve over mashed potatoes.

Servings: 4

<u>Ingredients</u>

¼ cup unbleached all-purpose flour

2½ cups chicken broth

8 bone-in chicken thighs, skin removed

2 tablespoons unsalted butter

2 stalks celery, finely diced

2 teaspoons dried parsley

½ cup dry white wine or water

1 large onion, peeled and diced

1 teaspoon dried thyme

12 ounces baby carrots, cut in half

1 bay leaf

1 recipe dumplings

½ teaspoon salt

¼ teaspoon freshly ground black pepper

Preparation

1. Put the flour, salt and pepper in a large zip-closure plastic bag and shake to mix.

2. Remove fat from chicken and add to the bag, seal and shake well to coat the chicken in the seasoned flour.

3. Melt the butter over medium-high heat in the pressure cooker. Add 4 chicken thighs once the butter starts to bubble and brown on each side for 3 minutes.

4. Transfer chicken to a plate. Add the remaining thighs and brown as usual. Remove to the plate. Add the celery and sauté for 2 minutes. Add the thyme and onion; sauté until the onion is softened.

5. Stir in the parsley, carrots, broth, water or wine and bay leaf. Bring the browned chicken thighs (along with their juices) back to the pressure cooker.

6. Lock the lid and bring to high pressure for 10 minutes. Quickly release the pressure and remove the lid. Remove the bay leaf and discard.

7. With the pressure cooker still on the heat, adjust it to maintain a simmer. Drop full teaspoons of the dumpling batter into the simmering stew. Cover a little to allow a small quantity of the steam escape and cook for about 15 minutes.

<u>Dumpling Batter</u>

1. In a mixing bowl, add 2 cups of unbleached all-purpose flour, 1 tablespoon of baking powder, and ½ teaspoon of salt. Stir well.

2. With two forks or a pastry blender, cut in 5 tablespoons of unsalted butter. Add 1 large beaten egg and ¾ cup buttermilk, stirring until the mixture comes together.

Seafood Chowder

Clam juice is salty. If using it in this recipe, wait until after tasting for seasoning then you may add salt. Serve with a tossed salad and dinner rolls.

Servings: 6

<u>Ingredients</u>

4 cups fish broth or clam juice

6 medium- sized russet or Idaho baking potatoes, peeled & diced

1 pound scrod or other firm white fish

2 tablespoons butter

½ cup heavy cream

2 large leeks

1 bay leaf

½ teaspoon dried thyme

2 cups water

Salt & freshly ground black pepper, to taste

<u>Preparation</u>

1. Melt the butter over medium heat in the pressure cooker. Cut the root end of the leeks off and throw away any bruised outer leaves. Slice and add leeks to the pressure cooker, sautéing for 2 minutes.

2. Stir in the potatoes, broth and water. Add the bay leaf, salt, pepper and then lock lid into place bringing to high pressure and maintaining this pressure for 4 minutes. Quickly release the pressure and take out the lid. Remove the bay leaf and discard.

3. Cut the fish into bite-size pieces. Add these pieces to the pressure cooker and simmer for 3 minutes. Add the cream and thyme. Bring the cream to temperature, stirring from time and time.

Lamb Stew Africana

Cinnamon simmering in orange juice generates an appetizing aroma that fills the kitchen. Your family will love you more for this dish. Serve with couscous.

Servings: 6

<u>Ingredients</u>

2 pounds boneless lamb shoulder

1 tablespoon olive or vegetable oil

1 cup dried apricots, quartered

2 cloves garlic, peeled and minced

1 large onion, peeled and diced

1/3 cup raisins

1 tablespoon fresh ginger, minced

1/3 cup blanched whole almonds

½ teaspoon ground cinnamon

¾ cup red wine

1/3 cup fresh mint leaves, packed

¼ cup fresh orange juice

Fresh mint leaves for garnish, optional

Salt and freshly ground pepper, to taste

Preparation

1. Bring the oil to temperature over medium-high heat in the pressure cooker. Trim lamb of fat and cut the meat into bite-size pieces.

2. In 4 batches, brown the lamb for 5 minutes each. Set aside the browned lambs and keep warm.

3. Set heat to medium. Add the onion and sauté it for 3 minutes. Add the garlic; sauté it for 30 seconds. Stir in the browned lamb.

4. Add raisins, apricots, ginger, almonds, wine, cinnamon, mint leaves and orange juice.

5. Secure lid and bring to high pressure for 20 minutes. Remove from heat. Allow natural release of pressure. Remove the lid. If desired, garnish with fresh mint.

Clam Chowder Manhattan

The clams and the clams liquid will be salty, so it's best to wait until the chowder is cooked before adding any salt. Serve with dinner rolls, oyster crackers, or toasted garlic bread.

Servings: 6

<u>Ingredients</u>

4 slices bacon

4 6½-ounce cans minced clams

4 large carrots, peeled and finely diced

2 stalks celery, finely diced

1 large sweet onion, peeled and diced

1 28-ounce can diced tomatoes

1 pound red potatoes, peeled and diced

2 cups tomato or V-8 juice

1/8 teaspoon dried oregano

½teaspoon freshly ground black pepper

1 teaspoon dried parsley

¼ teaspoon dried thyme

Sea salt, to taste

<u>Preparation</u>

1. Drain the clams and set aside, reserving the liquid to add together with the other liquid. Fry the bacon over medium-high heat and crumble.

2. Next, add the carrots and celery; sauté 3 minutes. Add onion; sauté 3 minutes. Stir in the potatoes, stir-frying to coat the potatoes in the fat. Stir in undrained tomatoes, clam liquid, juice, thyme, parsley, pepper and oregano.

3. Lock lid and bring to high pressure for 5 minutes. Set heat to warm and allow the pressure to drop for 10 minutes naturally. Quick-release remaining pressure, remove the lid and stir in the reserved clams. Bring to a simmer and season to taste.

Green Chicken Chili

Serve with tortilla chips or cornbread. Have sour cream, grated jack cheese or Cheddar and guacamole or avocado slices available at the table.

Servings: 8

Ingredients

3 pounds mixed meaty chicken pieces, skin removed

1 cup dried pinto beans

2 teaspoons vegetable oil

4 cups chicken broth

1 tablespoon olive oil

1 large carrot, peeled and diced

1 medium onion, peeled and diced

2 tablespoons unbleached all-purpose flour

2 jalapeño peppers, seeded and diced

2 medium red bell peppers, seeded and diced

4 cloves garlic, peeled and minced

1 chipotle pepper, seeded and diced

4 4-ounce cans chopped green chili peppers

8 cups water

2 tablespoons butter

Salt and freshly ground black pepper, to taste

Preparation

1. Begin by rinsing the beans and soaking them overnight in 3 cups of the water. The next day, drain water, add the beans, the remaining 5 cups of water, and vegetable oil to the pressure cooker.

2. Secure lid in place and bring to high pressure for 15 minutes. Remove and allow pressure to release on its own. Strain the beans and set aside. Wash the pressure cooker and dry.

3. In the pressure cooker, bring the olive oil to temperature over medium-high heat. Add the onion and sauté for 3 minutes. Add the carrot and sauté 3 minutes.

4. Stir in the jalapeño peppers and red bell; sauté until the vegetables are soft. Add the canned peppers, garlic, chicken pieces, chicken broth and chipotle peppers,

5. Close and bring to high pressure for 12 minutes. Quickly release the pressure. Transfer the chicken pieces to a bowl.

6. Once the chicken is cool enough to handle, trim the meat from the bones, cut into bite-size pieces, and put the meat back in the pressure cooker. Add the beans and stir.

7. Bring the chili to a boil and then mix the butter and flour together to make a paste. Whisk the paste into the chili.

8. Boil for 1 or 2 minutes and then lower heat to maintain a simmer until the chili is thickened. Add salt and pepper if necessary. Serve.

New Eng Clam Chowder

Serve with toasted, buttered sourdough bread or oyster crackers.

Servings: 4

<u>Ingredients</u>

4 slices bacon

4 6½-ounce cans chopped clams

2 large shallots, peeled and minced

2½ cups unsalted chicken or vegetable broth

1 stalk celery, finely diced

1 pound red potatoes, peeled and diced

1 tablespoon fresh thyme, chopped, optional

1 cup frozen corn, thawed

1 cup heavy cream

2 cups milk

Sea salt &freshly ground black pepper, to taste

<u>Preparation</u>

1. Drain the clams but reserve the liquid and set aside. Fry the bacon over medium-high heat and crumble.

2. Add celery and sauté 3 minutes. Add shallots and sauté for 3 minutes. Add the potatoes; stir-frying to coat the potatoes in the fat. Add the clam liquid, thyme, broth and then stir.

3. Close and bring to high pressure for 5 minutes. Reduce the heat to warm and let the pressure drop naturally for 10 minutes. Quickly release any remaining pressure and then remove the lid.

4. Stir in the milk, corn, reserved clams and cream. Bring to a simmer for 5 minutes.

Old South Chicken Stew

The sugar in this meal offset the tomatoes' acidity. With the aroma of the bacon fat, you will be transported back to a time when Southern cooks kept a bacon drippings container at the ready.

Servings: 8

Ingredients

1 10-ounce package frozen whole kernel corn, thawed

8 chicken thighs

3 tablespoons bacon fat

1 10-ounce package frozen okra, thawed & sliced

1 28-ounce can diced tomatoes

2 large yellow onions, peeled and sliced

¼ teaspoon sugar

1 10-ounce package frozen lima beans, thawed

½ cup dry white wine or chicken broth

1 cup bread crumbs, toasted

Salt and freshly ground black pepper, to taste

3 tablespoons Worcestershire sauce

Hot sauce, to taste, optional

2 cups water

Preparation

1. In the pressure cooker over medium heat, bring the bacon fat to temperature. Add 4 chicken thighs with the skin side down and fry until lightly browned.

2. Remove the fried chicken thighs and fry the remaining thighs. Bring back the first 4 fried chicken thighs to the pressure cooker and then add the tomatoes, water, wine or chicken broth, onions and sugar.

3. Lock into place and bring to high pressure; maintaining pressure for 12 minutes. Quickly release the pressure and take out the lid. Remove the chicken.

4. Remove the meat from the bones once it is cool enough to handle and discard the skin and bones. Shred meat and set aside.

5. Add the okra, corn and lima beans to the pot. Bring to a simmer and cook for 30 minutes uncovered. Stir in the bread crumbs, Worcestershire sauce and shredded chicken.

6. Simmer for 10 minutes, stirring infrequently to bring the chicken to temperature and to thicken the stew. Add hot sauce if desired and salt and pepper if needed.

Barley and Lima Bean Soup

Barley and lima beans make this colorful soup very hearty and give it a luscious, thick texture. Be sure to use baby limas, which have different cooking requirements than large ones—no presoaking required.

Servings: 6

Cups: 12

<u>Ingredients</u>

1 cup dried baby lima beans

3 tablespoons olive oil, divided

1 ½ cups onions, coarsely chopped

3 ribs celery, sliced

4 cups water

4 cups low-sodium vegetable or chicken broth

½ cup pearl barley

1 (15-ounce) can diced tomatoes, including juice

1 ¼ teaspoons dried Italian herb blend

4 large carrots, trimmed and scrubbed (leave whole)

1 small bunch kale (thinly slices stems, coarsely chopped leaves)

1 to 2 teaspoons balsamic vinegar

½ cup grated Parmesan or Romano cheese, plus more if desired

Salt, to taste

Preparation

1. In a 6-quart pressure cooker, heat 2 tablespoons olive oil then add the celery and onions, cooking over medium-high heat and stirring regularly until the onions are lightly browned.

2. Pour in the broth (standing back to avoid hot oil), tomatoes and water. Stir in the beans, dried herbs, kale stems and barley.

3. Add the kale leaves (use the back of a large spoon to press well into the liquid). Place carrots on top. (If necessary, cut carrots in half crosswise so it fits.)

4. Lock the lid and bring to high pressure for 20 minutes. Lower the heat to maintain the pressure and set on high for 15 minutes.

5. Turn off the heat and allow the pressure release naturally for about 10 minutes. Quick-release the remaining pressure. Remove the lid carefully.

6. Cut a few beans in half to check for doneness; they should be one color all through. If the beans aren't thoroughly cooked, simmer the soup uncovered for 3-4 more minutes until done.

7. Use a long knife to slice the carrots into chunks. Add remaining 1 tablespoon of oil and stir. Season with salt and balsamic vinegar.

8. Divide among 6 bowls. Garnish individually with cheese. Serve the remaining cheese at the table.

Simple Pinto Beans

Ingredients

1 pound dry pinto beans

1 bunch cilantro stems, tied with butcher's twine

1 small onion, finely chopped

7 cups water

1 garlic clove, minced

1 1/2 teaspoons salt

1 teaspoon ground cumin

Preparation

1. Add all the ingredients in the pressure cooker, cover, lock lid and cook on 40 minutes for high pressure.

2. Release completely. Open the pressure cooker lid and serve.

Chard, Butternut, & White Bean Soup

Servings: 6

Ingredients

16 ounces dried white beans

3 large carrots, chopped medium

1 tablespoon olive oil

3 stalks celery, chopped

1 large onion, chopped

1 sprig fresh rosemary, minced

4 sprigs fresh thyme

8 cups chicken stock

Pepper

2 cups diced butternut squash

1 teaspoon fresh rosemary, chopped

4 cups of chopped Swiss chard leaves

4 garlic cloves, sliced

1 -2 cup of chicken stock for thinning soup

Salt & pepper

1 cup crouton

1/2 cup sour cream

Preparation

1. In a pressure cooker, heat 1tablespoon of olive oil, sauté onion, carrot and celery until softened. Do not let brown.

2. Add in rosemary sprig, chicken stock, white beans, pepper and thyme sprig. Bring pressure to 15lbs and cook for 35 minutes until the beans are almost soft. Quick-release pressure and open lid.

3. Add in garlic, butternut squash, rosemary, salt & pepper to taste. Cover and cook for another 10 minutes. Release pressure naturally. Stir in chard greens and serve. If soup is too thick, thin with the remaining chicken stock.

4. Check to ensure beans are fully soft. Remove stems of thyme and rosemary. Add salt if needed. Serve with a dollop of sour cream& croutons.

White Bean Chili Pie

Servings: 8-10

Ingredients

2 medium tomatoes, chopped

2 cups cooked ham, cubed

1 cup frozen corn kernels

1 onion, chopped

1 envelope taco seasoning

1 red pepper, chopped

2 cans diced tomatoes with green chilies (Rotel brand)

1 pound dry white beans, rinsed & drained

2 cups water

Preparation

1. Sort and rinse beans with cold water then add to the pressure cooker. Next, add the water and all other ingredients.

2. Following your pressure cooker directions, simply cook under pressure for 50 minutes. Open lid and serve.

South American Black Bean Soup

Servings: 6

<u>Ingredients</u>

1 pound dried black beans, soaked overnight, rinsed & drained

2 tablespoons extra virgin olive oil

1 red bell pepper, chopped

1 large red onion, chopped

5 garlic cloves, minced

1 teaspoon ground cumin

1 bay leaf

2 teaspoons dried oregano

1½ teaspoon salt

1 teaspoon black pepper

2 tablespoons sherry vinegar

4 cups water

½ cup red wine

Garnishes:

Chopped tomatoes

Chopped red bell pepper

Finely chopped red onion

Chopped avocado

Minced scallion

Preparation

1. In a 5 quart pressure cooker, heat oil and then add onion, garlic, red bell pepper, bay leaf, oregano and cumin.

2. Sauté about 5 minutes until onions are soft. Add pre-soaked beans, vinegar, black pepper, red wine, salt and water.

3. Cover securely. Bring to high pressure, lower heat and cook on high pressure for 15 minutes. Turn off heat. Allow pressure release for 15 minutes naturally. Release any pressure that is left. Remove lid.

4. If desired, partially blend beans in soup with an immersion blender. Serve with assorted garnishes.

Green Beans & Bacon

Serving: 4-8

Ingredients

8 cups fresh green beans

1/2 lb bacon, thickly sliced

1/8 cup sugar, more or less to taste

Salt and pepper, to taste

Preparation

1. Wash beans, add to the pressure cooker then add water to just cover it. Secure lid into place and set timer for 5 minutes. Meanwhile, in a small fry pan, chop and brown bacon until crispy then set aside.

2. After 5 minutes, release pressure. Add the bacon including the grease and the sugar. Stir, close lid and set for 5 more minutes.

3. Season with salt and pepper then serve.

Black Bean Soup& Smoked Turkey
Servings: 8

<u>Ingredients:</u>

1 smoked turkey drumstick, discard skin & cut meat into bite size pieces.

2 cups dried black beans

1/2 tbsp extra virgin light olive oil

1 carrot, chopped

1 large onion, chopped

1 celery stalk, chopped

3 garlic cloves

1/2 cup chopped parsley

6 cups water

2 bay leaves

1/4 tsp fresh ground black pepper

1 1/4 tsp kosher coarse salt

<u>Preparation</u>

1. In a 6 quart pressure cooker, heat the olive oil then add onions, parsley, celery and carrots, cooking over medium high heat for about 10 minutes. Now add the garlic and cook for another 1 minute.

2. Add bay leaves, black pepper, turkey leg, water and beans and bring to boil. Cover and lock the lid. Bring pressure cooker to high pressure. To maintain pressure, lower heat to medium-low and cook for 45 minutes.

3. Turn off heat. Let pressure release naturally. Remove lid, set aside and discard bay leaves. Set turkey legs aside.

4. using an immersion blender, puree the beans to your desired consistency. Add salt and bring the turkey back to the soup. Ladle soup into 8 bowls

BBQ Baked Bean
<u>Ingredients</u>

1 1/2 cup dry navy beans, sorted and rinsed

4 slices of bacon sliced into approx 1/4" wide pieces

6 cup water

2 bay leaves

1 cup onion, chopped

2 cloves garlic, diced

1/4 cup green pepper, diced

1/4 cup Dijon mustard

1/4 cup molasses

1/4 cup tomato paste

1/2 cup brown sugar

2 tablespoon soy sauce

2 tablespoon BBQ Sauce

2 tablespoon hot sauce

1 tablespoon chili powder

1 tablespoon Worcestershire sauce

1 teaspoon seasoned salt

2 whole cloves

Preparation

1. In a pressure cooker, place beans, water and bay and bring to high pressure for 15 minutes. Quick release pressure. Keep 2 cups of cooking liquid aside and drain beans. Return beans and 2 cups liquid to pressure cooker. Discard bay.

2. Cook bacon in a large skillet until it is crisp. Place bacon on a paper towel; remove all but 1 tablespoon of bacon fat. Add the onion and cook for 3-4 minute. Add garlic and cook for another minute. Turn off heat and add everything else to skillet, mixing well.

3. Pour over the beans but do not stir. Return to high pressure for 10 minutes then quick release pressure. Remove the cloves. Serve.

Sausage, Cranberry Bean And Kale Stew
Servings: 4

Ingredients

3 links uncooked sausage, cut into 1-inch slices

1 tablespoon extra-virgin olive oil

1 small onion, chopped

1 clove garlic, minced

2 cups cranberry beans, soaked

1 bunch (about 2 1/2 cups) fresh kale, chopped

32 ounces low-sodium chicken broth

1 dried bay leaf

Salt and pepper

Preparation

1. In a pressure cooker, heat olive oil over medium heat. Add onion, sauté until translucent. Add sausage, sauté about 5 minutes until sausage is browned.

2. Add garlic, sauté and stir 30 seconds. Add beans, bay leaf and kale. Pour the chicken stock into pot and mix well.

3. Lock lid into place, bring to high pressure over high heat and set timer for 10 minutes. Lower the heat to maintain pressure and then remove cooker from heat after 10 minutes.

4. Now, release heat naturally. Remove lid carefully. Remove bay leaf. Add salt and pepper to taste.

White Beans The New Orleans Style
Servings: 8

Ingredients

1 pound great northern beans, dried

2 ribs celery

1 small green pepper

4 cloves garlic, minced

1 medium onion

2 bay leaves

1 tablespoon soy sauce (or gluten-free tamari)

1 teaspoon dried thyme

1/2 teaspoon white pepper

1 teaspoon dried oregano

1 teaspoon salt

Tabasco, to taste

Hickory smoked salt, to taste (optional)

Preparation

1. Soak beans overnight or quick-soak by putting them into the pressure cooker with water to cover them by just three inches. Bring to high pressure, cook for 1 minute and naturally release pressure before opening the cooker.

2. Drain soaking liquid. Place the beans into cooker. Add 5 cups water to it and heat, uncovered. Set to Brown.

3. Meanwhile, in a food processor or by hand, chop all vegetables fine, adding to the pressure cooker as you chop. Add other ingredients except Tabasco and the hickory smoked salt, if using.

4. Check the water level in the pressure cooker and add 1 more cup if there isn't enough water to cover all the ingredients by 1 inch.

5. Cover and set the timer for 12 minutes or bring to high pressure, cooking for 12 minutes. Turn off cooker, and the let pressure come down naturally.

6. Check beans for doneness. If beans are still tough, return to high pressure for a few minutes. If tender, add Tabasco and smoked salt, sauté uncovered on low until the liquid reduces and the cooking water starts becoming more like a sauce.

7. Stir frequently so they don't burn. If the liquid still seems watery after about 20 minutes, remove bay leaf and blend part of the beans with an immersion blender. Add salt to taste. Serve over hot rice with hot sauce placed on the table.

Pressure Cooker Potato Recipes

Potatoes With Fresh Parsley

Servings: 4

Ingredients

2 lbs potatoes, peeled &sliced

1 cup water or chicken stock

2 Tbsp fresh parsley, minced

4 Tbsp butter, cut into cubes

Salt& pepper to taste

Preparation

1. Place potatoes and parsley into pressure cooker and stir. Season with salt and pepper. Add water or chicken broth and top with butter.

2. Lock lid securely and cook for 6 minutes on high. Release pressure quickly. Remove and serve.

Potato & White Leek Soup

Servings: 8

Ingredients

4 large potatoes, peeled and sliced

2 tablespoon butter

1 medium onion, chopped

3 medium leeks (white portion only), sliced

1 liter chicken stock

2 cups light cream or milk

2 tablespoons fresh parsley, minced

Salt & pepper to taste

<u>Preparation</u>

1. In the pressure cooker, sauté the onions and leeks in the butter until tender. Add stock and potatoes. Secure cover. Bring to full pressure over high heat. Lower heat to medium-high and cook 5 minutes.

2. Remove from the heat. Cool immediately according to manufacturer's directions until pressure is completely reduced.

3. Uncover pot; cool soup a little. In batches, process soup in a blender until smooth. Bring back all to the pan. Add parsley and cream; heat through over medium-low heat but do not boil. Add salt and pepper, to taste.

Mashed Potatoes With Green Onions

<u>Ingredients</u>

2 pounds Yukon gold or russet potatoes, peeled & cut into 1/2 inch thick slices

4 green onions, trimmed & thinly sliced

3/4 cup milk

4 tablespoons butter

2 teaspoons kosher salt

Preparation

1. In the pressure cooker, melt butter over medium heat; add the green onions and potatoes. Sprinkle with the salt, toss to coat with the butter and pour the milk into the pot, stirring well.

2. Lock the lid cooker, bring it to high pressure and cook at high pressure 7 minutes.

3. Quick-release the pressure, open the lid away and mash the potatoes. If too thick, add a little more milk. Add more salt if needed.

Crunchy Roast Potatoes

Ingredients

4-5 tablespoon Vegetable Oil

1-2 lbs (500g - 1k) Baby or Fingerling Potatoes

1 sprig rosemary

3 Garlic Cloves (outer skin on)

½ cup stock

Salt& Pepper to taste

Preparation

1. Heat vegetable oil in the pressure cooker. Add the potatoes, rosemary and garlic. Roll the potatoes around, brown for about 10 minutes on all sides.

2. using a sharp knife, make a pierce in the middle of each potato. Pour in the stock. Secure lid lock the lid of and cook at high pressure for 7 minutes. Release pressure naturally.

3. Remove garlic cloves' outer skin. Sprinkle with salt and pepper to taste and serve!

Quick Mashed Potatoes

Enjoy this creamy and rich yet light and fluffy potato dish

Servings: 4 - 6

<u>Ingredients</u>

2 lbs. Russet potatoes

1 ½ - 2 cups milk, cream or half and half

 Butter or margarine, optional

Salt to taste

<u>Preparation</u>

1. Peel the potatoes, remove any eyes and green in the skin or under the peel, if any. Remove about 1/16th inch of the outside of the potato. Rinse briefly under cold water. Cut each potato into large chunks of about 2".

2. Add 1 cup of cold water and vegetable steamer to the pressure cooker bowl. Place potatoes above the steamer, ensuring the food doesn't rise above the cut-off line displayed on your pressure cooker. Cook at high pressure for 7 minutes. Quick Release.

3. Open lid carefully. Remove the potato chunks. Discard any waterlogged bits. Heat the milk in the pressure cooker using the "browning" setting.

4. Add butter to the milk, 1 tablespoon per cup of milk, if desired. Once milk has plenty of little bubbles around the edges with steam rising from it, turn off heat.

5. Process or mash the potatoes until soft and easily fall apart. Add part of the hot milk. Slowly stir the hot milk into the potatoes until fully absorbed. Repeat until the potatoes attain the desired consistency. Add salt to taste.

Pressure Cooker Rice & Risotto Recipes

Confetti Rice

Brown rice makes for a healthy, fiber-rich dish so use instead of white rice, if desired.

Servings: 6

Ingredients

3 cups frozen mixed vegetables, thawed

1 cup long-grain white rice, rinsed & drained

1 small red onion, peeled& diced

3 tablespoons butter

2 cloves garlic, peeled & diced

¼ cup fresh lemon juice

1 14-ounce can chicken broth

1 tablespoon ground cumin or herb blend

½teaspoon freshly ground black pepper

½ teaspoon salt

Preparation

1. In the pressure cooker, melt the butter, set to medium heat. Add the onion and sauté until soft. Add the garlic and then sauté it for 30 seconds.

2. Add the rice, stirring to coat in the butter; sauté until the rice becomes translucent. Add all other ingredients. Stir well.

3. Secure the lid into place; bring to high pressure for 7 minutes. Remove and allow pressure to release on its own. Remove the lid. Fluff rice with a fork. Taste and add seasoning if necessary.

Veggie Risotto With Beet Greens

To make this a vegetarian meal, substitute vegetable broth or water for the chicken broth.

Servings: 4

Ingredients

1 clove garlic, peeled & minced

¼ cup extra virgin olive oil

1 medium onion, peeled, thickly sliced

1 small Asian eggplant, sliced

1 portobello mushroom

1 small zucchini, sliced

2 cups young beet greens, sliced

1 large red bell pepper, seeded & cut in quarters

Salt and freshly ground black pepper, to taste

¼ cup butter

2 cups chicken broth

1 cup Arborio rice

½ cup dry white wine

½ cup Parmigiano-Reggiano cheese, grated

¼ cup fresh basil, sliced

Preparation

1. Add the garlic and oil to a small bowl; stir and set aside to infuse the garlic's flavor into the oil. Leave for 10 minutes.

2. Meanwhile, preheat the grill over medium-high heat. Remove the black gills and stem from the mushroom cap and slice the cap.

3. Brush sides of the eggplant slices, bell pepper quarters, zucchini slices, onion and mushroom slices with the oil. Place vegetables in the grill pan. Add salt and pepper to taste.

4. Turn once, grilling the vegetables on each side for several minutes or until slightly charred and softened. Set aside to cool. Coarsely chop.

5. Bring the rest of the garlic-infused oil and 3 tablespoons butter to temperature over medium heat in the pressure cooker.

6. Add the rice, stir to coat in the oil-butter mixture and then stir in the broth and wine.

7. Lock the lid and bring to high pressure for 7 minutes. Remove cooker, quick-release the pressure and remove lid.

8. Add the chopped grilled vegetables, basil and beet greens. Cover the pressure cooker without locking the lid into place.

9. Let it rest, covered, until greens are wilted. Add cheese, remaining butter and stir. Taste for seasoning. Add more salt and pepper to taste.

Brown Rice Green Salad

This main-dish salad is best served with honey-mustard dressing over salad greens. You may also experiment with different flavors.

Servings: 6

<u>Ingredients</u>

4½ cups chicken broth

2 cups long-grain brown rice, rinsed & drained

1 whole chicken breast, skin removed

1½ teaspoons salt

2 large carrots, peeled and diced

3 green onions, finely diced

2 stalks celery, sliced

2 hard-boiled eggs, peeled & chopped

1 small red bell pepper, seeded& diced

1 teaspoon Dijon mustard

3 tablespoons mayonnaise

1 teaspoon honey

2 tablespoons apple cider vinegar

2 tablespoons butter, melted

½ cup extra virgin olive oil

2 tablespoons fresh parsley, finely chopped

Salt and freshly ground white pepper, to taste

Preparation

1. Add the chicken, rice, broth and salt to the pressure cooker. Secure the lid and bring to high pressure for 12 minutes.

2. Remove pot from heat, quick-release the pressure, remove the lid and move the chicken to a cutting board. Fluff rice with a fork and place in a bowl.

3. Once cooled, toss rice with the onions, celery, bell pepper and carrots.

4. To make the dressing, combine the mayonnaise, honey, mustard, vinegar and melted butter, whisking well. Whisk in the olive oil slowly.

5. Fold in the chopped boiled egg. Add salt and pepper to taste. Add honey if desired.

6. Pour half dressing over the rice- salad mixture in the bowl, stirring to mix. Add more dressing if needed. Sprinkle parsley over the salad and serve.

Succulent Coconut Rice

Enjoy this succulent rice dish. It is really good served with a curry entrée.

Servings: 4

Ingredients

1 cup extra long-grain white rice, rinsed &drained

2 tablespoons butter or vegetable oil

½ cup unsweetened coconut, flaked or grated

¼ cup currants

2¼ cups water

1/8 teaspoon ground cloves

½ teaspoon ground cinnamon

1 teaspoon anise seeds

½ teaspoon salt

Preparation

1. In the pressure cooker, bring the oil or butter to temperature over medium heat. Add the rice, stirring to coat it in the fat.

2. Add the water, coconut, cinnamon, currants, anise seeds, cloves and salt. Secure lid and bring to high pressure, maintaining the pressure for 3 minutes. Turn heat off and let the pressure drop on its own for 7 minutes.

3. Release any remaining pressure quickly and remove the lid. Fluff rice with a fork. Drain off excess moisture. Add seasoning as needed. Serve.

Sweet Brown Rice Risotto

The white grape juice concentrate makes the rice real sweet. If you' want to keep it absolutely savory, do away with the white grape juice concentrate and use ¼ cup of white wine and 2½ cups of water instead.

Servings: 8

Ingredients

2 cups short-grain brown rice, rinsed& drained

2 medium leeks

3 tablespoons butter

1 small fennel bulb

½ teaspoon salt

1½ teaspoons freshly ground or cracked black pepper

2¾ cups water

¾ cup Fontina cheese, grated

1 tablespoon frozen white grape juice concentrate

<u>Preparation</u>

1. Cut the leeks lengthwise into quarters, and then slice into ½-inch slices; wash well, drain, and dry.

2. Clean, trim the fronds from the fennel and chop. Dice the bulb.

3. In the pressure cooker, melt the butter over medium heat. Add the fennel and leeks; sauté for 1minute.

4. Add the rice, stir-fry into the almost wilted leeks until the rice starts to turn golden brown. Add the water, white grape juice concentrate and salt.

5. Secure lid and bring to high pressure for 20 minutes. Take it out from the heat and let pressure release for 10 minutes naturally. Quick-release any pressure left. Remove the lid.

6. Fluff rice with fork. Stir in the fennel fronds, cheese, and pepper. Taste and add more salt if necessary. Serve.

Lime Rice With Chipotle's Cilantro
<u>Ingredients</u>

1 cup long grain rice

1 tablespoon fresh lime juice

2 tablespoons vegetable oil

3 tablespoon fresh chopped cilantro

1 teaspoon salt

1 1/4 cups water

Preparation

1. Add the rice, 1 tablespoon oil, salt and water to the pressure cooker. Stir. Lock lid in place and select high pressure for 3 minutes.

2. Turn off pressure cooker off. Naturally release pressure for 7 minutes then quick release pressure. Fluff rice with a fork.

3. Combine lime juice, chopped cilantro and1 tablespoon oil in a medium bowl. Add rice and toss until well mixed.

Pressure Cooker Desserts

Tea Poached Pears
Servings: 4

Ingredients

2 slices lemon

3 Earl Grey tea bags tied together

4 firm pears, peeled not cored,

1/4 tsp vanilla essence

2 cups water

2 cinnamon sticks

1/2 cup sugar

Preparation

1. In the Pressure Cooker, mix together water, lemon, sugar, tea bags, vanilla essence and cinnamon sticks. Simmer until the sugar dissolves.

2. Next, place the pears in the Pressure Cooker even if they don't stand upright. Cover lid securely and bring pressure to high-heat then reduce heat and cook for 8 minutes.

3. Remove from heat. Release pressure quickly and then use a skewer to check the level of the softness of the pears. If more cooking is needed, replace lid and bring back to pressure to cook for two more minutes.

4. Transfer the pears to a large bowl with a slotted spoon and discard the tea bags. Boil sauce to lessen until it is syrupy. Drizzle over the pears and serve with cream, custard or ice cream.

5. (To make in advance, cool the pears and place in a container. Pour the syrup over the pears and then seal container. To serve, remove pears from container, heat in the microwave for 2 minutes on medium setting. Heat the syrup separately for 1 minute in the microwave).

Chocolaty Rice Pudding

Servings: 6-8

Ingredients

1 1/2 cups Arborio rice

200g dark chocolate, chopped

1/3 cup caster sugar

6 cups milk

1 tsp vanilla extract

50g butter

1/4 teaspoon ground chili, optional

Preparation

1. Put the rice, butter, milk, sugar and vanilla, into the Pressure Cooker and stir.

2. Close lid into place and bring to high pressure

3. Once at pressure, turn down the heat and cook for 8 minutes.

Cob Corn Plain

You'll love this dish if you're watching your calories! This tastes delicious without any salt or butter.

Servings: 4

Ingredients

1 lime, quartered

4 ears fresh sweet corn, shucked

Freshly ground black pepper, to taste

½ cup water

Preparation

1. Place the rack in the cooker and then place the corn on the rack. Pour the water in.

2. Lock the lid and bring to low pressure for 3 minutes. Remove from heat, quick-release the pressure and remove the pressure cooker lid.

3. Transfer to 4 serving plates. Squeeze a wedge of lime juice over corn and season each ear of corn with grind black pepper.

Orange Zest Cornmeal Cake

Servings: 4

Ingredients

¼ cup light brown sugar, packed

2 cups milk

1 teaspoon orange zest, grated

1 large egg

½ cup fine yellow cornmeal

2 egg yolks

2 tablespoons orange marmalade

2 tablespoons butter, melted

1 cup water

Preparation

1. Bring the milk to a simmer over medium heat. Add the brown sugar; stir, simmer and stir again until milk is at a low boil.

2. Whisk in the cornmeal and orange zest. Simmer, stir for 2 minutes and then remove from heat. Combine the egg, egg yolks, marmalade, butter and orange and whisk into the cornmeal mixture.

3. Treat a 1 quart soufflé with nonstick spray. Add batter. Pour the water into the pressure cooker and add rack. Place the soufflé dish on the rack.

4. Secure lid and bring to low pressure, maintaining pressure for 12 minutes. Remove from the heat and let the pressure release on its own. Quick-release the pressure that is left and remove the lid. Transfer to a wire rack.

Pearl Tapioca Pudding

This dish can be combined with other flavors. It may be stirred with some toasted pecans, coconut or chocolate chips and served with a dollop of whipped cream.

Servings: 4

<u>Ingredients</u>

½ cup small pearl tapioca

1/3 cup sugar

1cup water

2 large eggs

1 tablespoon butter

1/8 teaspoon salt

1 cup heavy cream

1½ cups milk

1 teaspoon vanilla

<u>Preparation</u>

1. In a small bowl, combine the tapioca and water; cover and soak overnight. Add the butter, sugar, salt and eggs to a bowl, beating until smooth.

2. Stir in the cream, milk and vanilla. Drain the soaked tapioca and add to the milk mixture and stir.

3. Coat a 1-quart stainless steel bowl with spray (nonstick). Pour the tapioca mixture into the bowl. Tight bowl with heavy-duty aluminum foil.

4. Pour the rest of the cup of water into the pressure cooker, add the rack and crisscross long, doubled strips of foil over it to create handles to remove the pan later.

5. Center the pan, still covered, holding the tapioca mixture on the foil strips on the rack.

6. Secure lid and bring to low pressure for 12 minutes. Remove from the heat, quickly release the pressure and remove the lid.

7. Lift the pudding from the pressure cooker. Allow to rest for 15 minutes, remove the foil cover and stir. Add more vanilla if desired. Refrigerate until ready to serve.

Yummy Steamed Dessert Bread

Serve this steamed dessert bread with sweetened cream cheese or butter. To toast leftovers, simply place slices on the oven rack for 5 minutes in a 350°F oven.

Servings: 8

<u>Ingredients</u>

½ cup stone-ground cornmeal

½ cup unbleached all-purpose flour

½ cup of whole wheat flour

Butter

¼ teaspoon fine salt

½ teaspoon of baking powder

½ cup buttermilk

½ cup maple syrup

1 large egg

2 cups water

¼ teaspoon of baking soda

Preparation

1. Add the cornmeal, flour, baking powder, whole wheat flour, baking soda and salt to a mixing bowl. Stir to mix.

2. Add the buttermilk, egg and maple syrup to another mixing bowl. Whisk and then pour into the flour mixture. Mix until thick batter forms.

3. Butter a 6-cup baking pan. Add batter to fill it. Butter one side of a piece of heavy-duty aluminum foil to cover the baking dish top. Place the buttered foil side down over the pan and seal by crimping the edges.

5. Pour the water. Place the rack into the cooker. Crisscross long, doubled foil strips over the rack to create handles for removing the pan later.

6. Place pan on the rack over the strips of foil. Lock the lid and bring to low pressure for 1 hour. Take it out from heat; let the pressure release of its own accord.

7. Remove the lid. Lift pan from cooker and place on a cooling rack. Remove foil.

8. Use a toothpick to test the bread; if the inserted toothpick comes out wet, place foil over pan and return to the pressure cooker to cook for a longer time. If the bread is done, loosen the bread with a knife and invert it on the cooling rack. Serve warm.

CPSIA information can be obtained
at www.ICGtesting.com
Printed in the USA
FSOW01n0910010816
23312FS